NONE DARE CALL IT
ISLAM

Why the President and the Media Ignore
the Truth About Our Radical Enemy

NONE DARE CALL IT ISLAM

JOHN RABE

D. James Kennedy
MINISTRIES™
TRUTH IN *Action* ®

Fort Lauderdale, FL

NONE DARE CALL IT ISLAM
Why the President and the Media
Ignore the Truth About Our Radical Enemy

By John Rabe

ISBN: 978-1-929626-51-9

Jacket and Interior Design: Roark Creative, www.roarkcreative.com

Published by:
    D. James Kennedy Ministries
    P.O. Box 7009
    Albert Lea, MN 56007
    1-800-988-7884
    www.DJamesKennedyMinistries.org
    letters@truthinaction.org

Printed in the United States of America

CONTENTS

INTRODUCTION

"ISIL is not 'Islamic.' No religion condones the killing of innocents, and the vast majority of ISIL's victims have been Muslim...it has no vision other than the slaughter of all who stand in its way."

— President Barack H. Obama,
September 11, 2014

President Barack Obama, speaking to the nation from the Oval Office on the 13th anniversary of the 9/11 attacks on America, repeats a theme that has become a hallmark of his administration's foreign policy: that those committing violent atrocities in the name of Islam are not actually Islamic.

The president insistently uses the acronym ISIL (Islamic State in Iraq and the Levant—"Levant" being a rather arcane term referring to the general region) to describe the organization, though it is far more well known as ISIS (Islamic State in Iraq and Syria).* But in either case, "Islamic" appears directly in the group's name. Nationwide, millions of mouths drop in astonishment at President

---

* The reasons for this are unclear, but many in the media speculate that it is because the Obama Administration does not want to include "Syria" because of Obama's previous decision not to get involved in the struggle for power between rival factions there. See "'ISIS' vs. 'ISIL' vs. 'Islamic State': The political importance of a much-debated acronym," Jaime Fuller, Washington Post, September 9, 2014.[1]

Obama's seemingly absurd statement. After all, ISIS has been killing in the name of Allah, has declared a caliphate—or Islamic kingdom—in Syria and Iraq, has announced plans to spread the caliphate into Europe and Africa, and called upon Muslims worldwide to submit to it.[2] In a very short amount of time, ISIS has drawn hundreds of thousands of radical Muslims to its cause, steamrolling through Iraq and Syria in the course of a few months to take control of the vast majority of territory in each nation.

Like most Americans, I am astonished at President Obama's refusal to name the enemy. As I listen, I realize there can be only one of two possibilities: either the president is breathtakingly ignorant of reality, or he has hidden political and philosophical reasons for fudging the obvious truth.

I do not believe President Obama is an ignorant man. Nor is he alone in his refusal to acknowledge the obvious truth about radical Islamic terrorism. Indeed, the mainstream media has been complicit, seemingly obfuscating the truth at every turn. And this did not begin with President Obama (though he seems to have virtually made it an art form). It actually began in the previous presidential administration, under George W. Bush.

The fact is that there is an ongoing, conscious attempt—almost always at odds with the facts—to dissociate terrorism done in the name of Islam from some supposed Platonic ideal of Islam in which violence is never done, diversity is welcome, and peace rules the day. Such an ideal "Islam" is a chimera. While it is absolutely true that the majority of Muslims in the world are peaceful people who do not engage in violence or terrorism, such acts can by no means be considered part of some tiny fringe that only nominally uses the name "Islam" as a cover.

In addition, while it is also true that Muslims are often the victims of radical Islamic terrorism, President Obama's attempt to use this as evidence for his assertion that such violence is not part of "Islam" is a non-sequitur. The fact that there has been much violence done within Islam among different sects, each claiming to be more faithful to "true" Islam than the others, actually *refutes* the president's argument rather than *supporting* it.

To anyone whose eyes are open, the nature of radical Islam, displayed on nearly every continent, is all-too-readily apparent. Just as the very words of this introduction are being written (on February 4, 2015):

- The world is in shock over video released within the past 24 hours of a Jordanian pilot being burned alive by ISIS.

- Three French soldiers have been stabbed while patrolling outside a Jewish community center in Nice, France. The attacker is identified as Moussa Coulibaly, who was expelled from Turkey a week earlier because he was believed to be seeking to join ISIS. According to *The New York Times*, "The attack coincided with the emergence of a video by the Islamic State militant group inciting French jihadists to carry out further terrorist acts."[3]

- Zacarias Moussaoui, the so-called "20th hijacker" of 9/11 has given a sworn statement in a civil case saying that members of the Saudi royal family helped finance Al Qaeda.[4]

- Islamist insurgent group Boko Haram attacked military camps in Fotokol, Camaroon, killing 17 people.[5]

And in just the past week as of this writing:

- At least 32 people were killed in Egypt in a series of jihad attacks on police and soldiers.[6]

- A suicide bomber, believed to be working at the behest of the Taliban, killed at least a dozen people and injured 39 others at a funeral in Mehtar Lam, Afghanistan.[7]

- Jundullah, a splinter group of the Pakistani Taliban, attacked a mosque in Pakistan, killing 55 and wounding 59.[8]

And this is just a partial list. The situation is unlikely to be much different on the day that you are reading this. Pick virtually any day at random, and you will be able to find news of dozens of deaths (or more) because of radical Islamic terror attacks worldwide.

Yet the Obama Administration continues to insist that none of this has to do with "true" Islam, that such attacks have "no vision" and are driven by no religious ideology—by nothing more than a basic thirst for violence.

In September 2014, Fox News reported on an appearance by Secretary of State John Kerry before a congressional committee in regard to ISIS. Kerry's testimony showed just how far the administration will go to divorce terrorism from Islam of any kind:

"They're not a state, and they do not represent Islam," Kerry said in testimony before the House Foreign Affairs Committee.

At several points during the hearing, Kerry sought to describe the group in other terms. He called them a "militant cult masquerading as a religious movement." At another point in the hearing, he used the phrase "Islamic radical groups" but immediately corrected himself.

"Islamic is the wrong word—radical religious extremists," he clarified.[9]

No one in the administration has explained how President Obama and Secretary Kerry—neither of whom are Islamic theologians—are able to discern what is "true" Islam and what is not, given all the world's various Islamic factions.

In January 2015, an Islamic militant, Amedy Coulibaly, assaulted a Jewish kosher supermarket in Paris, France, killing four people. Coulibaly left behind a video pledging allegiance to ISIS, detailing how the attack was planned by multiple people. French police charged four members of an Islamic cell group for collaborating with him.[10]

Yet, in an interview a month later with *Vox.com*, President Obama said:

> It is entirely legitimate for the American people to be deeply concerned when you've got a bunch of violent, vicious zealots who behead people or randomly shoot a bunch of folks in a deli in Paris.[11]

"Randomly shoot a bunch of folks at a deli in Paris." Every piece of evidence shows that the attack was the furthest thing from random—that it was, in fact, a planned attack targeted at Jews because of Islamic motivations and was carried out by Muslims. Still the president, with a straight face, refers to it as a random attack.

How many such "random" attacks—which are occurring daily, with great bloodshed across the world, will have to happen in order for the President of the United States to call Islamic terrorism by name? It almost defies explanation. Like the famous (and hilarious) Monty Python pet shop sketch, in which an aggrieved owner attempts to return his dead bird only to have the shop owner firmly and repeatedly deny that the stone-cold, unmoving, stiff bird is dead ("He isn't dead; he's pining for the fjords"), the president refuses to admit what is plain and obvious to everyone else paying attention. Except that when human lives are in danger, it is not funny.

This book is an attempt to examine this phenomenon: the strange reality that when it comes to radical Islamic terrorism in the world today, in our government and media, *None Dare Call It Islam*.

CHAPTER ONE

MEDIA CONTORTIONS

The mainstream media has a long history of reluctance to identify radical Islamists as the culprits in a whole host of atrocities, while at the same time being quick to pin major crimes on innocent parties.

Much like the government, it seems that many in the media reflexively adopt the government line that Islamic terrorism has nothing to do with "true Islam."

In 2014, there was an interesting argument on Bill Maher's live HBO television show between actor/director Ben Affleck and Maher, a liberal comedian who has been outspoken on Islamic terrorism. The heated discussion also included the atheist author Sam Harris, a critic of Christianity who more recently has been speaking out on the effects of Islam.

Maher began by commenting on the liberal values that were largely missing from Islam, such as freedom of speech, freedom of religion (including the freedom to leave the religion of Islam), and equality for women.[12]

Harris made the valid point that American liberals will get quite agitated about abortion clinic attacks that took place back in 1984, but are largely silent on cultural Islam. He added, "We have been sold this meme of Islamophobia where every criticism of the doctrine of

Islam gets conflated with bigotry towards Muslims as people."[13]

That is when things got heated. Affleck immediately proved Harris' claim correct by taking umbrage with his characterization, leading to the following discussion:

AFFLECK: How about more than a billion people who aren't fanatical, who don't punch women, who just want to go to school, have some sandwiches, pray five times a day, and don't do any of the things you're saying of all Muslims. It's stereotyping.

HARRIS: I'm not saying all Muslims—

AFFLECK: Some of them do bad things and you're painting the whole religion with that broad brush.

MAHER: Wait, let's get down to who has the right answer here. A billion people, you say.

AFFLECK: A billion five.

MAHER: All these billion people don't hold these pernicious beliefs?

AFFLECK: They don't.

MAHER: That's just not true, Ben. That's just not true. You're trying to say that these few people, that's all the problem is, these few bad apples. The idea that someone should be killed if they leave the Islamic...

AFFLECK: That's horrible.

MAHER: But you're saying the idea that someone should be killed if they leave the Islamic religion is just a few bad apples?

AFFLECK: The people who would actually believe in that you murder someone if they leave Islam is not the majority of Muslims at all...[14]

As detailed later in this book [see chapter 3, "True Islam"], majorities of Muslims in major nations like Egypt, Pakistan, Jordan, Afghanistan, Malaysia, and also in the Palestinian territories, totaling into the hundreds of millions of people, do in fact believe that apostates from Islam should be executed.[15]

But Affleck, who perhaps ought to know better, considering that he directed an Oscar-winning film about the violent Islamic revolutionary takeover of Iran and the U.S. Embassy there in 1979 leading to the Iran hostage crisis, nevertheless continued on with his counter-attack:

AFFLECK: Your argument is, "You know, black people, they shoot each other"—

MAHER: It's not! No, it's not. It's based on facts. I can show you a Pew poll of Egyptians. They are not outliers in the Muslim world. It's like 90 percent of them believe death is the appropriate response to leaving the religion. If 90 percent of Brazilians thought that death was the appropriate response to leaving Catholicism you would think it was a bigger deal.[16]

What was most telling about this exchange was the media's reaction to it. The media almost universally lined up behind Affleck, who was proffering the preferred narrative, despite not marshaling many facts to his defense.

After a report on the exchange during CBS *This Morning* a few days later, which portrayed Maher as "controversial" and Affleck as charitable, co-host Gayle King said, "It makes me want to go back and look at the whole thing. I thought Ben Affleck was raising some really good points. You just can't paint everybody with the same brush."[17]

The Huffington Post chimed in with "Why Ben Affleck Is Right,

Bill Maher Is Wrong, And Sam Harris Is Jaded About Islam."[18]

Peter Beinart took to the website of *The Atlantic* to decry "Bill Maher's Dangerous Critique of Islam."[19]

A student group at the University of California-Berkeley organized a petition drive to disinvite Maher from speaking at the school's winter commencement because of his "hate speech."[20]

Affleck was said to have "blasted"[21] Maher's "racism," and was hailed for his "passionate defense of Islam."[22]

Among the mainstream media (which in many ways is merely a subset of American liberalism), there is one narrative allowed: violence and Islam have no real connection, so acts of violence should never be attributed to Islam. Instead, other causes must be found, and other people must be blamed. Examples of these alleged perpetrators comprise quite a list.

The Beltway Snipers

For several weeks in 2002, John Allen Muhammad and his accomplice, Lee Boyd Malvo, terrorized the greater Washington D.C. area as the so-called Beltway Snipers. The pair shot 13 people, killing ten, over the course of three weeks. As it turned out, they had also killed as many as five others (and wounded six more) around the country in cities ranging from Tacoma, Washington to Montgomery, Alabama.

On the day the pair were identified, a chase and standoff ensued. That entire evening, the broadcast and cable news networks tried to avoid using John Muhammad's adopted (and legal) surname "Muhammad" and instead kept calling him "John Allen Williams." This, despite the fact that he had officially converted to Islam in 1997, immediately began calling himself "Muhammad," and had his name legally changed in 2001.[23]

The networks scrambled to cite Muhammad's Gulf War I experience, abuse as a child, and hatred for a spouse as possible motives for the shootings. CBS's Vince Gonzalez reported the next day, "About the same time he joined the army Muhammad converted to Islam, but authorities say religion was not a motive."[24]

Subsequent evidence definitively proved that the shootings were carried out as an act of jihad. Malvo, Muhammad's accomplice, had also converted to Islam[25] and while awaiting trial he drew hundreds of sketches in prison that ultimately became evidence. One of them depicted Osama Bin Laden with a police officer in sniper's sights, and the caption, "We did not start this flame, we merely picked up the torch." On another drawing, he wrote, "I have been accused on my mission. Allah knows I'm gonna suffer now."[26] On yet another drawing, Malvo wrote, "THIS IS WAR. IT WILL GO ON AND ON UNTIL YOU ARE TOTALLY DESTROY [sic], YOUR [sic] WHITE STATE OF MIND... HOLY WAR! JIHAD."[27]

The Fort Hood Massacre

In 2009, Nidal Malik Hasan, a Muslim who was a U.S. Army major and psychiatrist, opened fire at his base in Fort Hood, Texas, killing 13 and wounding 32 others.

Despite the fact that many who knew Hasan noted that he was becoming more radicalized as a Muslim, had been in touch with radical Islamic imam (and Al Qaeda sympathizer) Anwar al-Awlaki,[28] was increasingly vocal in his anti-war, anti-American statements, and was shouting "Allahu akbar" (Arabic for "Allah is great") when he opened fire, the networks speculated that perhaps he was suffering from post-traumatic stress disorder, which motivated the shootings.

The only problem: Nidal Hasan had never been deployed to a war zone.

The media then shifted gears and speculated that it was "secondary" PTSD—an entity entirely of their own creation—resulting from his work as a psychiatrist talking to *others* who had been deployed.[29]

A study of network television coverage of the Fort Hood shootings by the Culture and Media Institute showed that discussion of Hasan's terrorist sympathies was mostly absent from the three major broadcast networks' news programs in the five days following the shooting. The report noted that 93 percent ignored his terror connections and 85 percent of the network reports never used the word "terror."

The media were not the only ones to turn a blind eye toward Hasan's real motives. The United States government itself followed suit. [See also chapter 3, "The Obama Administration's Blind Eye."].

But why is this? Could it be, perhaps, that the members of the media, who above nothing else should want to get the facts right, were just being extremely circumspect and in their abundance of caution were endeavoring not to jump to premature or unwarranted conclusions?

As the French say, "It is to laugh."

In fact, the record shows that members of the media will actually *race* each other to speculate about possible conservative (and Tea Party) involvement in major crimes. When any conceivable opportunity arrives to do so, they throw caution to the winds.

A few representative examples:

Times Square Car Bomb

On May 1, 2010, police foiled an attempted car bombing on a Saturday night in New York City's packed Times Square.

Shortly after the attempted attack, then-Mayor Michael Bloomberg appeared on the *CBS Evening News* with Katie Couric. He said it was not yet known who the attacker was, but he had some thoughts:

KATIE COURIC: Law enforcement officials don't know who left the Nissan Pathfinder behind, but, at this point, the mayor believes the suspect acted alone.

MAYOR MICHAEL BLOOMBERG: If I had to guess 25 cents, this would be exactly that, somebody—

COURIC TO BLOOMBERG: A home-grown?

BLOOMBERG: Home-grown, maybe a mentally deranged

person or somebody with a political agenda that doesn't like the health care bill or something. It could be anything.[30]

Couric did not challenge Bloomberg's theory that the attack was motivated by opposition to Obamacare, but the facts eventually did. It turns out it could *not* have been "anything" after all.

Shortly after Bloomberg's comments on CBS, the perpetrator was identified as Faisal Shahzad, who had emigrated from Pakistan and had become an American citizen. He was traced through the serial number on the parked car, which was packed with explosives and was in the beginning process of detonating. Shahzad nearly escaped, but was apprehended on a United Arab Emirates flight to Dubai as it sat on the tarmac about to take off from a New York airport.

Despite the imaginary profile Bloomberg offered, it turned out that Shahzad was not mentally deranged, was not an opponent of the health care bill, and was not working alone. Not by a longshot. In fact, Bloomberg could hardly have been more spectacularly—or predictably—wrong. As ABC News reported:

Accused Times Square Bomber Faisal Shahzad linked up with the Pakistani Taliban through the internet, ABC News has been told by law enforcement and intelligence sources close to the investigation. Once the Taliban identified him as more valuable in the U.S. than in Pakistan, they trained him to return to execute his bomb attack.

But according to these sources, Shahzad also had a web of jihadist contacts that included big names tied to terror attacks in the U.S. and abroad, including the figure who has emerged as a central figure in many recent domestic terror attempts—radical American-born Muslim cleric Anwar Awlaki.[31]

Yet another case of Islamic terrorism falsely chalked up to opponents of the Obama administration.

Gabrielle Giffords' Shooting

On January 8, 2011, Congresswoman Gabrielle Giffords (D-Arizona) and 18 other people were shot by Jared Lee Loughner during a public appearance at a supermarket in Tucson. Giffords was critically injured but survived, while 6 others (including a nine-year-old girl) were killed.

Loughner was taken into custody at the scene, and within minutes, the media rushed to blame...Sarah Palin. Why? Because "targeting" imagery featuring crosshairs had been used in some Republican campaign ads arguing for the vulnerability of Giffords' congressional seat.

CBS News breathlessly reported in the hours after the attack:

We do not yet know what prompted 22-year-old accused gunman Jared Loughner to allegedly shoot Rep. Gabrielle Giffords (D-Ariz.) and others, including a child and federal judge who died from their wounds.

But critics of Sarah Palin have already drawn a link between the shooting and the fact that the former Alaska governor put Giffords on a "target list" of lawmakers Palin wanted to see unseated in the midterm elections.[32]

Leftist actress Jane Fonda agreed, tweeting, "Progressive Arizona Rep. Gabrielle Giffords is shot. In her ads, Sarah Palin had her targeted in a gun site. Inciting to violence."[33] It was later demonstrated that Democratic candidates had used the target imagery, quite common in politics, in equal proportion to the Republicans.

New York Times columnist Paul Krugman, writing the weekend of the shooting, joined many in blaming general air of incivility and "toxic rhetoric" for the shootings, asking:

Where's that toxic rhetoric coming from? Let's not make a false pretense of balance: it's coming, overwhelmingly, from the right... Listen to Rachel Maddow or Keith Olbermann, and you'll hear a lot of caustic remarks and mockery aimed at Republicans. But you won't hear jokes about shooting government officials or beheading a journalist at *The Washington Post*. Listen to Glenn Beck or Bill O'Reilly, and you will.[34]

As laughably tendentious as Krugman's claims were (the very liberal Olbermann, for example, included a daily segment on his MSNBC program in which he named some conservative "The Worst Person in the World"), they were common coming from the media in the days immediately following the shootings.

But while trying to pin-the-tail-on-the-conservatives, the media almost completely ignored the actual facts that emerged in the days following the shootings. In college, Loughner became fascinated with nihilism, which is the philosophy that says that everything is ultimately meaningless. The father of nihilism was Friedrich Nietzsche, who coined the famous phrase, "God is dead" and was a powerful figure for such leftist philosophers as Michel Foucault and Jacques Derrida (who are among the fathers of today's postmodernism). Nietzsche was the furthest thing from a conservative.

Three years earlier at a public event, Loughner (echoing Nietzsche) stood up and asked Rep. Giffords, "What is government if words have no meaning?"[35] That is a chilling—and perfectly rational— question for someone in the thrall of leftist deconstructionism to ask.

Strangely, once it became clear that Loughner could not be tied to Republicans or the Tea Party, the media stopped talking about him. When they thought (hoped?) he was a conservative, there was no thread too thin with which to tie his ostensible political viewpoint to the crime. No holds were barred as they speculated in every conceivable way about how he was probably driven by conservative hate.

Yet, when his actual beliefs came out and turned out to represent a radically leftist view of the world, the media was no longer interested in connecting his political viewpoint to his actions. His course no longer fit the preferred narrative, so it was jettisoned.

Of course, it is quite likely that Loughner was simply insane. But if he had any identifiable political positions, they were of the Left. A friend of his in the days after the attacks tweeted that Loughner was "very liberal" and added, "he was leftwing when I knew him in hs [sic] & college, 3 years ago."[36]

While he gave no indication that he was driven by talk radio or campaign ads, he gave *many* indications that he could have been driven by a philosophy of meaninglessness that is still widely taught on many college campuses. But the media was not nearly as interested in following the implications that were actually *there* in front of them as they were in announcing the ones that they had *invented*—which were later disproved.

Aurora, Colorado Theater Shooting

In Aurora, Colorado, on July 20, 2012, James Holmes walked into a midnight premiere of the Batman film *The Dark Knight Rises* and opened fire, killing 12 and injuring 70.

Just a few hours later on ABC's *Good Morning America*, investigative reporter Brian Ross had found a "Jim Holmes" from Colorado on Facebook and was eager to tell a waiting nation about his findings. As Jack Mirkinson in the liberal *Huffington Post* described the scene:

> George Stephanopoulos threw to him on *Good Morning America* by saying, "You've been investigating the background of Jim Holmes here. You found something that might be significant."

> "There's a Jim Holmes of Aurora, Colorado, page on the Colorado Tea party site as well, talking about him joining the Tea Party last year," Ross said. "Now, we don't know if this is the same Jim Holmes. But it's Jim Holmes of Aurora, Colorado."[37]

Alas, it was not the same "Jim Holmes," and Ross would fail to win a Pulitzer (or an Emmy, or even a Peabody award) for his scattershot Facebook search reported via a major network news program. He did, however, win ABC News the distinction of having to issue a formal apology for the incident.

In actuality, Holmes turned out to be a very troubled young man who had attempted suicide several times, had "middle-of-the-road" political views, was obsessed with the lethal "Joker" character from the Batman films, and had no political motive for the shootings.[38]

Boston Marathon Bombings

On April 15, 2013, two homemade pressure-cooker bombs exploded at the finish line of the Boston Marathon, killing three people and injuring hundreds of others. The bombers were discovered to be brothers Tamerlan and Dzhokhar Tsarnaev, Chechen refugees to America who had become radical Muslims[39] and had jihadist motives for the attack.[40]

In the hours after the attack, the media was indeed very cautious not to speculate about possible *Islamic* terrorism. They were more than forthcoming when it came to speculating about *other* possibilities, however.

Literally just moments after the bombings, CNN's Wolf Blitzer, broadcasting live, wondered aloud:

> One intriguing notion, one intriguing thought here…it is a state holiday in Massachusetts today called Patriots' Day, and uh, who knows if that had anything at all to deal…to do with these explosions.[41]

NBC's Luke Russert took an early opportunity in a tweet to connect the shootings with the Branch Davidian assault years before, which had angered some militia groups:

> I was at Fenway Park w my dad and @mikebarnicle during Waco which was on Patriots Day in 1993. Speculating on possible link.[42]

(There turned out to be absolutely no connection between Waco and the Marathon attack, meaning the only potentially true information in this tweet is that young Luke Russert took in a Red Sox game in April 1993.)

Chris Matthews of MSNBC, never reticent to jump off the cliff of speculation, wondered in the hours immediately after the bombing if it was perpetrated by a conservative tax protester:

> Normally domestic terrorism people tend to be on the far right, although that's not a good category. Let's just… extremists, let's just call them that.[43]

Later Matthews remembered that it was April 15, leading to even more speculation:

> I just forgot because I filed already—that it's filing day for the federal income tax, which does cause some emotions around the country, sometimes in the wrong parts of the brain…[44]

The mainstream media has proven over and over again that they will rush to judgment—almost always inaccurately—if they see an opportunity to impugn conservatives, Christians, the Tea Party, or anyone else they perceive as being on the right. And yet when it comes to Islam, no matter how high the stack of evidence gets, no matter how much an attack fits the pattern, no matter the facts of recent history, the media will pretend that Islam had nothing to do with it until they simply cannot pretend any longer.

The members of the media fancy themselves the "guardians" of freedom, keeping an eye on government and looking out for the people. But by purposely obfuscating and turning a blind eye to real threats to the American people, they are abdicating their responsibilities as journalists in favor of partisan posturing. Their pre-chosen ideological prejudices so blind them that they often can no longer see the truth, even when it stares them in the face.

CHAPTER TWO

THE OBAMA ADMINISTRATION'S BLIND EYE

While the media's campaign to whitewash the violence of radical Islam is serious, the efforts of the United States government to do so are far more serious. Both the U.S. Constitution and the Bible (see Romans 13) charge government with the task of protecting the people from violent threats. When the government will not recognize the threat—and even seems to go to great lengths to deny the threat—it is serious business.

This is not a partisan problem, either. President George W. Bush established the precedent in the days after 9/11 and during the wars in Iraq and Afghanistan of claiming that Islam is "a religion of peace." He claimed often, without much in the way of evidence, that those who committed terrorist acts under the name of Islam had "hijacked" the religion.

One typical example occurred in remarks regarding humanitarian aid to Afghanistan in 2002. President Bush said:

> Islam is a vibrant faith. …We respect the faith. We honor its traditions. Our enemy does not. Our enemy doesn't follow the great traditions of Islam. They've hijacked a great religion.[45]

Whether or not violence is a departure from "the great traditions of Islam" is examined more closely later in this book [see chapter 4, "True Islam"]. But the point being made here is that the effort to separate terrorist acts from Islam itself was underway well before Barack Obama's arrival on the scene.

But while the Bush administration often employed the "religion of peace" trope in an effort to build and maintain a coalition of majority-Muslim nations for the Iraq and Afghanistan wars, there's no doubt that the Obama administration has taken it to new, and often absurd, levels. And as President Obama's campaign to arbitrarily separate Islamic violence from Islam has continued apace, an increasing number of Americans has become concerned about the Obama administration's ability to deal with a problem they refuse to name.

Fort Hood

Perhaps the most egregious example of the government's whitewash of Islamic terrorism occurred in the wake of the 2009 Fort Hood massacre. As chronicled in the previous chapter, Army major Nidal Malik Hasan, the Muslim doctor who had been in email contact with senior Al Qaeda leader Anwar al-Awlaki, killed 13 fellow soldiers while shouting "Allahu akbar" (the Arabic phrase common to Muslims meaning "Allah is great").

The U.S. Defense Department, which, it should also be noted, is the department directing the military in the "War on Terror," commissioned a report dealing with the response to the shootings and how future such incidents could be prevented. In the report, the shootings are not dealt with as domestic terrorism but rather they were characterized as an incidence of "workplace violence."[46]

The report strives to find ways of identifying and dealing with future threats within the ranks. It analyzes "Indicators that DoD [Department of Defense] Personnel May Become a Threat to Themselves and Others," and "Barriers and Constraints on Taking Action," yet Hasan's ties to Islamic terrorism and professed Islamic motivations are never once mentioned in the 86-page document.[47]

Furthermore, the Pentagon doubled down on their stance that the attack was merely a case of "workplace violence" by refusing to award Purple Hearts to any of the 32 injured survivors.

Not until 2015, more than five years after the incident, did Obama's Defense Department quietly change its course after a ruling by Congress expanded the rules for who could receive a Purple Heart in order to include Fort Hood victims. The DoD then announced it would begin awarding Purple Hearts to Major Hasan's victims.[48] In doing so the department tacitly acknowledged—though they still will not *officially* acknowledge—that the attack was something more than "workplace violence."

Benghazi

On September 11, 2012, Islamic militants attacked the U.S. diplomatic compound and another nearby compound in Benghazi, Libya, killing four Americans including U.S. Ambassador Chris Stevens. The attack—and the United States' response to it—has become one of the most controversial issues of President Obama's administration.

The significance of the date chosen for the assault, which was the 11th anniversary of the 9/11 attacks on America, was not lost on most Americans. However, in his remarks in the Rose Garden the next morning, just hours after the U.S. ambassador had been killed, President Obama pointedly refused to characterize this attack as "terrorism."

Instead, for weeks the Obama administration insisted that the attacks were "spontaneous demonstrations" of anger against a YouTube video made in the U.S., which featured a demeaning portrayal of Islam's prophet Muhammad. As preposterous as this claim was—it should still have raised questions about a religion whose adherents would blithely kill Americans because of an internet video clip produced by an Egyptian-born American citizen. Making the rounds of the Sunday morning talk shows days after the fact, then-U.N. Ambassador Susan Rice pushed the administration's line. Her appearance on Fox News Sunday with Chris Wallace was representative:

The information, the best information and the best assessment we have today is that in fact this was not a preplanned, premeditated attack. That what happened initially was that it was a spontaneous reaction to what had just transpired in Cairo as a consequence of the video. People gathered outside the embassy and then it grew very violent and those with extremist ties joined the fray and came with heavy weapons, which unfortunately are quite common in post-revolutionary Libya and that then spun out of control.[49]

It was later shown that the attacks, far from being "spontaneous," were led by several Al Qaeda operatives. Furthermore, Al Qaeda leader Ayman al-Zawahiri had released a video the day before the assault calling for attacks on Americans in Libya to avenge the death of another senior Al Qaeda operative.[50]

Although President Obama would later falsely claim in an October 17, 2012 presidential debate that he *did* call the attacks "terrorism" in his immediate September 12 remarks, the record showed otherwise. (His remarks astonished his challenger Mitt Romney, who was then further astonished when moderator Candy Crowley of CNN jumped into the debate on the president's side— an event unprecedented in a presidential debate—and erroneously affirmed that Obama had indeed called the attack "terrorism.) An interview conducted with President Obama by CBS News' Steve Kroft of *60 Minutes* on the afternoon of September 12, 2012—just hours after his Rose Garden remarks—proved that the president's omission was intentional and purposeful.

KROFT: Mr. President, this morning you went out of your way to avoid the use of the word "terrorism" in connection with the Libya attack. Do you believe that this was a terrorist attack?

OBAMA: Well it's too early to know exactly how this came about, what group was involved, but obviously it was an attack on Americans.[51]

Far from denying Kroft's premise that he went out of his way not to use the word "terrorism," Obama *affirmed* Kroft's framing of the question, just hours after the attacks, by again repeating the notion that the American government did not know who did it.

In fact, the Obama Administration would not admit that the attack in Benghazi was a terror attack until two full weeks after the incident, long after there was any real question left about it.

Perhaps just as amazingly, the American public did not get the full truth in the run-up to the 2012 election. For weeks after the incident, as the Obama administration increasingly drew fire for its refusal to characterize the attack as terrorism—and even after Candy Crowley misled the American people during the presidential debate—CBS News stunningly kept that portion of the Sept. 12 interview with Steve Kroft secret. They had "smoking gun" proof of President Obama's intentions in his Rose Garden speech, and withheld it until just two days before the election, far too late to make any difference.

However, CBS News did assure Americans that the network's coverage of Benghazi was not influenced in the least by the fact that CBS News president David Rhodes is the brother of White House deputy national security adviser Ben Rhodes—who coordinated the Obama Administration's public response to the Benghazi attacks.[52]

Paris Deli Attacks

As noted in the introduction, President Obama sparked outrage after referring to a targeted jihadist attack on Jews at a kosher supermarket in Paris in January 2015 as "vicious zealots who… randomly shoot a bunch of folks in a deli in Paris."[53]

The man whom Obama says shot people "randomly," Amedy Coulibaly, was working with a radical Islamic terror cell and had left a video behind pledging his allegiance to ISIS. As Jonah Goldberg observes, this sort of willful obstinacy on President Obama's part begins to look like moral blindness the more often it is repeated:

There was nothing random about it, at all. There are about

310,000 Jews in the greater Paris area. Out of close to 12 million inhabitants. The odds of killing four Jews randomly are pretty daunting. But, thankfully, you don't have to do the math because Amedy Coulibaly said openly and proudly that he was targeting Jews. No one disputes this, except for Barack Obama. He would never describe the targeting of a black church by the Klan as simple random violence— nor should he. And we know he's perfectly comfortable denouncing crimes committed "in the name of Christ" no matter how ancient they may be. But crimes in the name of Allah must not be named as such—or at all.[54]

In the same interview, President Obama tipped his hand even further regarding his view on acts of Islamic terror. Addressing ISIS beheadings and the "random" shooting of Jews in France, he said:

It is right and appropriate for us to be vigilant and aggressive in trying to deal with that—the same way a big city mayor's got to cut the crime rate down if he wants that city to thrive.[55]

This, indeed, is central to President Obama's view of terrorism— and why his refusal to acknowledge reality is so dangerous for all of us. Goldberg is absolutely right to observe:

…not only is he refusing to describe the true nature of the threat, his rush to euphemisms causes him to analyze and describe terrorism incorrectly—as if Jihadism is analogous to street crime. This is not only morally obtuse, it is strategically daft. Street crime is bad. Terrorism is bad. But street crime and terrorism are not the same thing. We all agree that street crime shouldn't be treated like terrorism— no drone strikes for shoplifters! Why is it so hard to see the reverse is true? Terrorism shouldn't be treated like robbery.[56]

The Danger of Ignorance

On January 7, 2015, two gunmen stormed into the Paris offices of *Charlie Hebdo*, a French satirical newspaper that had gained international attention for printing cartoons making fun of Islam's prophet Muhammad.

Heard in videos shot from the street that were immediately uploaded to the internet, the gunmen shouted "Allahu akbar" as they ran out of the building. The attackers killed 11 people (including cartoonists and senior editors of *Charlie Hebdo*) and wounded 11 others inside, and also killed a police officer outside the building. Stephane Charbonnier, the newspaper's editor, had been included on a hit list in an Al Qaeda publication in 2013.[57]

Shortly after the attack, an Al Qaeda affiliate claimed responsibility for the attack, and announced that they had gained "revenge for the honor" of Muhammad.[58]

Yet the Obama administration once again refused to link "Islamic" and "terrorism."

Rep. Tulsi Gabbard, a Democratic congresswoman from Obama's home state of Hawaii who is also a veteran of the war in Iraq, spoke out in an interview with Fox News' Greta Van Susteren. Rep. Gabbard said that the refusal to name the enemy is putting national security at risk:

> This is not just about words. It's not about semantics. It's really about having a real, true understanding of who our enemy is and how important that is, that we have to understand what their motivation is and what their ideology is — the radical Islamic ideology that is fueling them.[59]

Senator Joe Lieberman, a former Democratic vice-presidential candidate, has said much the same thing.

> This is more than semantics. As military strategists since Sun Tzu have appreciated, the first rule in war is to know your enemy so you can defeat it.[60]

Obama's Secretary of State John Kerry, the official charged with carrying out the administration's foreign policy, has continued Obama's tack of attempting to separate Islamic violence from anything Islamic. In a speech to the World Economic Forum in Davos, Switzerland weeks after the *Charlie Hebdo* massacre, and in the midst of daily reports of atrocities committed by ISIS in the Middle East, Kerry raised the question of why someone might join up with an Islamic terror group:

> Well, the fact is there are a lot of explanations. Some say it's because of long-held cultural grievances—a sense that a person's creed or clan is under attack or has been disrespected or treated unjustly. Many point to the inclination to see the world in black and white terms and believe that they alone possess the truth. Others are lured by basic, material considerations—the promise of regular meals, a paycheck, the chance to plunder and loot. And then there are the mundane and personal choices: to escape boredom, go where the action is; be lured by a false sense of success; perhaps trade anonymity for notoriety, at least for a few hours, on the internet. In many cases, it's almost certainly a combination of these inputs.[61]

In other words, it has nothing to do with the tenants of Islam. It has to do with poverty, thrill-seeking, self-importance, or perhaps just too much certainty about the world.

Rep. Gabbard quickly dismissed that notion:

> If that's really the cause, then the solution would be just to give them a trophy, give them a hug, give them a good-paying job, $10,000, and a skateboard so they can go and get their thrills and say, "OK, great, they are going to be happy and they won't be fighting anymore." That's not the case. ... We've got to look at what their ideology is and how that's fueling these tragic attacks that keep on occurring.[62]

The refusal of the Obama administration to be clear about the ideology of the terrorists is not an imagined problem. Supporters of President Obama have portrayed this as a "shibboleth" issue, in which critics are merely trying to force the president to use a certain set of words to say what he has essentially already been saying. But there is a real issue at stake in the failure to name radical Islam as the culprit: it fits perfectly into the strategy of the jihadists.

As Dr. Walid Phares, who teaches global strategies at National Defense University in Washington D.C., has warned:

> ...[W]hen the intellectual defenses of a nation are put to sleep, its political institutions are unable to detect the threat....This [strategic] stage is "political mollification," which occurs when the opposing camp is successful in diverting the attention of the nation, its government, and its media from the prime enemy. The political influence of the opponent, backed with money, can blur the vision of the political establishment and paralyze its ability to become conscious of the mounting threat. The jihadist strategy aimed at anesthetizing the political establishment of the United States and the West in order to achieve its long-term objectives.[63]

Phares goes on to describe the further goal:

> The jihadi strategy is ultimately to be able to influence if not control U.S. foreign policy, and, subsequently, western policy toward the Middle East and the Arab and Muslim world.... But the gist of it—which usually escapes the public—is not a better adjustment to human rights, democracy, and freedom in the Arab and Muslim world: just the opposite. What the pro-jihadi critics demand is a further submission of Washington to antidemocracy policies in the region.[64]

Phares wrote those words in 2005, before Barack Obama was even president. Yet in the aftermath of the "Arab Spring," they look eerily prescient. Because President Obama insists on projecting a sunny view of Islam (in which "99.9 percent of Muslims... are looking for the same thing we're looking for—order, peace, prosperity") and because he insists that only a tiny fringe element hold violent, jihadist goals, he is caught by surprise when one nation after another in the Middle East falls into radical hands after he advocates regime change there.

Bad Diagnosis, Bad Cure

In a penetrating analysis of the Islamic State in Iraq and Syria in the March 2015 issue of *The Atlantic*, writer Graeme Wood observes:

The reality is that the Islamic State is Islamic. Very Islamic. Yes, it has attracted psychopaths and adventure seekers, drawn largely from the disaffected populations of the Middle East and Europe. But the religion preached by its most ardent followers derives from coherent and even learned interpretations of Islam.

Virtually every major decision and law promulgated by the Islamic State adheres to what it calls, in its press and pronouncements, and on its billboards, license plates, stationery, and coins, "the Prophetic methodology," which means following the prophecy and example of Muhammad, in punctilious detail. Muslims can reject the Islamic State; nearly all do. But pretending that it isn't actually a religious, millenarian group, with theology that must be understood to be combatted, has already led the United States to underestimate it and back foolish schemes to counter it.[65]

Examples of such "foolish schemes" are not hard to find. Indeed, State Department spokeswoman Marie Harf seemed to suggest during a round of talk show appearances in February 2015 that some sort of jobs program was ultimately the ticket to solving the ISIS problem. Appearing on MSNBC on *Hardball* with host Chris Matthews, the following exchange took place:

HARF: We cannot kill our way out of this war. We need in the medium to longer term to go after the root causes that leads people to join these groups, whether it's a lack of opportunity for jobs.

MATTHEWS: We're not going to be able to stop that in our lifetime or 50 lifetimes. There's always going to be poor people. There's always going to be poor Muslims, and as long as there are poor Muslims, the trumpet's blowing and they'll join. We can't stop that, can we?

HARF: We can work with countries around the world to help improve their governance. We can help them build their economies so they can have job opportunities for these people.[66]

Among other things, Harf's analysis (which is consistent with the statements of John Kerry and Barack Obama) overlooks the fact that Osama bin Laden, for example, hailed from a wealthy family, as did Mohamed Atta and a number of other prominent jihadists.

While it is undoubtedly true that there are socioeconomic factors that make joining groups like ISIS or Al Qaeda more appealing for some, and that retaliatory violence on its own is not likely a sufficient solution, it is difficult to miss Harf's obvious attempt to remove Islamic ideology completely from the equation.

This failure to recognize the religious motivation of ISIS also points to another ideological tilt of President Obama. As he works to separate acts of terrorism from "true Islam" and focuses instead on other factors (like "certainty," economic issues, supposed resentment from millennium-old events, etc.), he ignores the obvious. Wood notes in his piece for *The Atlantic*:

… focusing on [other factors] to the exclusion of ideology reflects another kind of Western bias: that if religious ideology doesn't matter much in Washington or Berlin, surely it must be equally irrelevant in Raqqa or Mosul.[67]

The increasingly radical leadership in Egypt, Syria, Iraq, Libya, Tunisia, Yemen, the rise of ISIS—all of this comes as a surprise to a president who exhibits a peculiar kind of blindness. As the old saying goes, there is none so blind as the one who refuses to see.

CHAPTER THREE

TRUE ISLAM

In the face of mounting contrary evidence, President Obama nevertheless continues to insist that Islamic violence has little to do with Islam itself. In an interview with CNN's Fareed Zakaria in the weeks following the bloody *Charlie Hebdo* attack in Paris and stepped-up assaults from ISIS in Iraq, Obama said:

> You know, I think that the way to understand this is there is an element growing out of Muslim communities in certain parts of the world that have perverted the religion, have embraced a nihilistic, violent, almost medieval interpretation of Islam, and they're doing damage in a lot of countries around the world.

> But it is absolutely true that I reject a notion that somehow that creates a religious war because the overwhelming majority of Muslims reject that interpretation of Islam. They don't even recognize it as being Islam, and I think that for us to be successful in fighting this scourge, it's very important for us to align ourselves with the 99.9 percent of Muslims who are looking for the same thing we're looking for—order, peace, prosperity.[68]

But compare this with the words from an editorial examining

"true Islam" in the *USA Today* the day after *Charlie Hebdo*:

> Contrary to popular misconception, Islam does not mean peace but rather means submission to the commands of Allah alone. Therefore, Muslims do not believe in the concept of freedom of expression, as their speech and actions are determined by divine revelation and not based on people's desires.

> … Muslims consider the honor of the Prophet Muhammad to be dearer to them than that of their parents or even themselves. To defend it is considered to be an obligation upon them. The strict punishment if found guilty of this crime under sharia (Islamic law) is capital punishment implementable by an Islamic State. This is because the Messenger Muhammad said, "Whoever insults a Prophet kill him."[69]

These words did not come from a *detractor* of Islam, but from Anjem Choudary, a prominent London Muslim cleric and lecturer in Sharia law.

President Obama has said elsewhere, "No religion condones the killing of innocents."[70] This sounds good—except that under many interpretations of Islam, including that of Muhammad himself—there are few if any non-Muslim innocents. Instead, the Koran says: "Slay the unbelievers wherever you come upon them, take them captives and besiege them, and waylay them by setting ambushes" (Surah 9:5).

The Koran advocates beheading unbelievers—in verses specifically cited by ISIS executioners:

> And when you meet in regular battle those who disbelieve, smite their necks; and, when you have overcome them, bind fast the …And if Allah had so pleased, He could have punished them Himself, but He has willed that He may try some of you by others. And those who are killed in the way

of Allah—He will never render their works vain. He will guide them and improve their condition, And admit them into the Garden which He has made known to them (Surah 47:5-7).

As Denis MacEoin, Distinguished Senior Fellow of the Gatestone Institute, who holds a Ph.D. in Persian/Islamic studies from King's College, Cambridge, notes:

Muhammad ordered or supported some forty-three assassinations of opponents, including several poets who had challenged him in verse. Better known are his reprisals against three Jewish tribes, two of whom were expelled from Medina, while the men of the third, the Banu Qurayza, were condemned to death by Sa'd ibn Mu'adh, whose judgement [sic] was endorsed by Muhammad. As many as 900 male members of the tribe—including boys of thirteen and upwards—were beheaded; the women and children were sold into slavery, or else the women were made concubines for the Muslim men. The Medinan period is nothing but rounds of violence piled on violence, all ordered or carried out by the "Prophet of Peace."[71]

These acts of Muhammad are particularly significant, because Islam of *any* stripe is not primarily a doctrinal religion. The Koran is seen as the divine revelation of Allah, but particular emphasis is placed on the activity of Muhammad. As Ron George, longtime missionary to Muslim countries, has said,

Islam is not a theological system. It's a legal system and so to know who you are, to know what to do, to know how to eat, where to live, how to travel, you always go back to Islamic law.

The heart of Islam is the Hadith and the Hadith is a collection of 600,000 sayings that developed over a 200-

year period. Now, between 650 and 850, various scholars traveled around the Muslim world—North Africa, Egypt, Palestine, Iraq—talking to people, collecting stories about what they understood Muhammad had said and what Muhammad had done. They collected these stories into a book called the Hadith and …now those stories tell you how to live your life.[72]

In other words, it could be said without stretching things too far that at the heart of Islam is the question, "What would Muhammad do?"

Furthermore, many in the west have tried to soft-peddle the concept of "jihad" (which means "struggle"), choosing to interpret it as a primarily inward, personal, spiritual struggle. Indeed, some Muslim sects have largely adopted this meaning for "jihad." But the well-established meaning of the word in history is far less sanguine.

Alvin J. Schmidt, retired professor of sociology at Illinois College, points out that:

Although the word "jihad" can indeed mean struggle or strive, it is quite another argument to say that it only means a personal struggle to improve one's spiritual life. Such an argument contradicts the majority of statements that speak about jihad in the Koran, the Hadith, and the Shariah, where the word almost exclusively means physical fighting and warlike activities done to advance a holy war(s) against the "infidels."[73]

Robert Spencer, who is the director of Jihad Watch and has been studying Islamic theology, law, and history for more than three decades, explains:

[T]here is a mainstream, an entrenched and indeed

dominant, Islamic tradition that teaches that warfare against unbelievers is the Koran's last word and most important word on jihad… jihad is warfare against unbelievers in order to subjugate them under the rule of Islamic law.[74]

As Spencer notes, Ibn Ishaq, the first biographer of Muhammad, writing in the 8th century, explained that the Koran's teachings on jihad had three stages of development. According to Ishaq, the first stage is tolerance, "which was the prevailing understanding of the relationship between Muslims and unbelievers during the period when Muhammad was in Mecca and the Muslims were small band, they did not have a whole lot of power, and were facing a much larger and more formidable enemy."[75] This is a stage of non-fighting, and is the stage to which the most peaceful verses in the Koran counseling patience and forbearance speak.

However, as Muslim power grows, there is a progression of stages, which each supersede the previous ones. In the second stage, Muslims are given permission to fight under certain circumstances. The final stage is offensive jihad, which *requires* fighting. Ishaq said this stage was now the permanent state dictated by the Koran to be followed at all times in the future.

Spencer observes, "[T]his is the unanimous teaching, actually, of the schools of jurisprudence and all the orthodox sects of Islam to this day, that offensive jihad is the highest level of jihad and the one that's applicable for all time."[76]

Dr. Walid Phares, a native of Beirut, Lebanon, is one of the premiere scholars on Islamic terrorism. He was NBC News' terrorism expert from 2003 to 2006, and now holds the same position with Fox News. Phares has written:

In the early 1990's, I was stunned to read and hear the western establishment making these tremendous efforts to convince audiences and readers of the benign character of jihad; in the Middle East, for the most part, the term retained its age-old, unreconstructed meanings. Jihad is not benign, and the West's denial of that fact was terribly ironic....The United States was paving the way for its own defeat....It was clear that the nation turned a blind eye to the historical definition of jihad, the one that would really come to matter.[77]

Some of the basic teachings of Islam, while perhaps denied by some modern day apologists, make this even clearer. For instance, there is the basic distinction between the House of Islam (*Dar al-Islam*) and the House of War (*Dar al-Harb*) which developed in early Islam and is maintained today. As the great scholar of Islam, Bernard Lewis, now professor emeritus of Near Eastern Studies at Princeton University, explains:

> One of the basic tasks bequeathed to Muslims by the Prophet was jihad. This word, which literally means "striving," was usually cited in the Koranic phrase "striving in the path of God" and was interpreted to mean armed struggle for the defense or advancement of Muslim power. In principle, the world was divided into two houses: the House of Islam, in which a Muslim government ruled and Muslim law prevailed, and the House of War, the rest of the world, still inhabited and, more important, ruled by infidels. Between the two, there was to be a perpetual state of war until the entire world either embraced Islam or submitted to the rule of the Muslim state.[78]

So while many Muslims today undoubtedly seek peace and eschew violence, who is being more faithful to the example set by Muhammad? And who can seriously claim that those seeking to follow Muhammad's violence with their own similar acts are "not Islamic?"

The "99.9 Percent"

The further problem with attempting to separate "Islam" from the "extremists" acting in its name is the avowed beliefs of the larger

Muslim world. President Obama says we must "align ourselves with the 99.9 percent of Muslims who are looking for the same thing we're looking for—order, peace, prosperity."

President George W. Bush, who initiated the war on terror made similar statements, often claiming that Islam is "a religion of peace."

It seems that our politicians and our media want to believe that the most liberal, Westernized, Americanized Muslims are representative of Islam as a whole, while those committing violence (or supporting such violence) are not. But a recent Pew survey[79] of Muslims in 39 countries in Europe, Asia, and Africa showed that while support of violence is indeed a minority view, it is a view with significant support. One struggles to compare President Obama's "99.9 percent" claim with the following figures:

Percent of Muslims who say suicide bombing is sometimes or often justified:

- Egypt: 29 percent (about 23.2 million people)

- Turkey: 15 percent (about 11.25 million people)

- Bangladesh: 26 percent (roughly 38.7 million people)

- Pakistan: 13 percent (about 23.5 million people)

- Afghanistan: 39 percent (about 11.9 million people)

- Malaysia: 18 percent (about 5.3 million people)

This represents well over 100 million people who believe suicide bombing is acceptable in some (or many) situations. And the survey did not even cover the nations of Iran, Syria, Nigeria, Sudan, Libya, Chad, and Saudi Arabia, which have either seen—or been party to—large flare ups of Islamic-driven violence.

In *no* nation surveyed was the number anywhere near

.01 percent—which President Obama essentially claims is the worldwide number of those "who are looking for the same thing we're looking for—order, peace, prosperity."

In fact, the survey found that right here in the United States, 19 percent of Muslims believed that suicide bombings affecting civilians are at least *sometimes* justified. That represents over a half million (of the estimated 2.7 million) Muslims living in America. Chilling numbers indeed.

Strangely, however, even the Pew Survey itself evidenced the kind of bias this book is examining. In reporting that over 500,000 Muslims in America are supportive of suicide bombings, the authors of the survey gave it an oddly optimistic phrasing:

> American Muslims are even more likely than Muslims in other countries to firmly reject violence in the name of Islam. In the U.S., about eight-in-ten Muslims (81 percent) say that suicide bombing and similar acts targeting civilians are never justified.[80]

One supposes an optimist could say that the glass is only 19 percent detonated.

This is indeed oddly sunny phrasing, especially considering that according to Pew the percentage of Muslims in America who believe suicide bombings are sometimes justified is actually *higher* than the percentage in Pakistan, Jordan, Indonesia, Morocco, and several other violence-torn nations.

The Historical Record

The historical record certainly does not favor the notion that "Islam is a religion of peace." Indeed, while again noting that not all Muslims are violent—nor are those advocating violence even the majority today—there is a systemic problem ingrained in Islamic theology, which often breeds violence. The historical evidence of more than a millennia's worth of incidents that have occurred in countless places is too overwhelming to ignore.

For many centuries violent Islamic expansionism and conquest has been the rule rather than the exception. While much attention is given to the Crusades as a blot on world history [see chapter 4, False Equivalences], the Crusades were, proportionately, a limited response to Muslim wars of aggressive conquest that took place in the first three centuries of Islam.

During that period, Muslim armies spread out from Arabia after the death of Muhammad to conquer territory in the name of Allah. They quickly moved through the Middle East, northern Africa, and large swaths of Asia, eventually reaching as far to the east as India. They even overran much of Europe, going as far west as Spain and as far north as France until they were repelled there by Charles Martel at the Battle of Tours in 732 A.D.

Additionally, Islamic armies launched attacks into Southern Italy, Sicily, Crete, Turkey, Austria, and were sometimes repelled and sometimes not, in the thousand years following Muhammad's death in 632 A.D.

From the very beginning, the religious followers of Muhammad waged offensive, territory-conquering, violent war on virtually all adjacent non-Muslim lands. And these wars were not merely coincidental to the Islamic religion. As Robert Spencer has written:

> What was the ultimate goal of this seemingly endless warfare? It is clear from the commands of the Qur'an and the Prophet, who told his followers that Allah had commended him, "to fight against the people until they testify that none has the right to be worshipped but Allah and that Muhammad is the Messenger of Allah." No Islamic sect has ever renounced the proposition that Islamic law must reign supreme over the entire world, and that Muslims must, under certain circumstances, take up arms to this end.[81]

Cultural Effects of Islam

In a multicultural world where relativism rules [see more in chapter 5], it is considered ill-mannered and politically incorrect to make judgments about cultures. But, as the philosopher and historian Richard Weaver wrote, ideas have consequences. The central ideas in a culture will determine the shape of that culture, for better or for worse, and religious ideas are most central of all. As some Christian theologians have noted, "Culture is religion externalized."[82]

It is absolutely true that the majority of the Muslim world is not involved in terror attacks. But even if we accept the assertions of George W. Bush, Barack Obama, John Kerry, and the media that these attacks do not represent "true Islam," what then are we to make of "true Islam?"

While those who might be considered "radical Muslims" are a minority in the Muslim world (though not a tiny minority, by any means), it is worth noting where mainstream, non-radical (in the terroristic sense) Islam takes a culture. Even if we pretend that violent jihad plays no role in true Islam, is Islam the tolerant, peaceful, uplifting religion that President Obama portrays?

Here are some facts about Muslim-dominant countries in which Sharia law plays some role (and adherence to Sharia law is one of the defining characteristics of all of Islam).

According to the 2013 Pew Survey, over 70 percent of Muslims in Malaysia, Thailand, Indonesia, Afghanistan, Pakistan, Bangladesh, Iraq, the Palestinian territories, Morocco, Egypt, Jordan, Niger, Djibouti, Congo, and Nigeria believe that Sharia law should be the law of the land.[83] And what about in nations where Sharia is the official law of the land? In 11 nations, Sharia law applies in full, backed by the civil government. Among these nations are Iran, Saudi Arabia, Sudan, Pakistan, and Yemen.

How do these fully Muslim nations, applying full Muslim law, do on issues of tolerance and peace?

Freedom of Religion

* Not one of the nations under Sharia law allows freedom of religion. For instance, there is not a single Christian church in all of Saudi Arabia. As noted by the international Christian relief group Open Doors International:

The desert kingdom is defined by Wahhabism, a purist and strict interpretation of Islam. It is forbidden to openly practice other religions. Apostasy—conversion to another religion—is punishable by death....Converts to Christianity from Islam face the risk of being killed or abused by their own families. House churches are often raided by the religious police.[84]

* Of the top 20 nations where Christian persecution is the worst on Open Doors International's Watch List, 16 of them are nations where Sharia law plays some part in governance. Two more are nations where Sharia plays no official role yet are majority Muslim. (The remaining two are communist dictatorships in North Korea and Vietnam.)[85] In other words, 90 percent of the top 20 worst persecutors of Christians are Muslim countries, most of which are governed to some degree by Sharia law.

* Sharia law calls for the execution of apostates who leave Islam, and modern Muslims who take Sharia seriously agree. The 2013 Pew survey of Muslims showed that "[I]n six of the 20 countries where there are adequate samples for analysis, at least half of those who favor making Islamic law the official law also support executing apostates."[86]

* After the downfall of Saddam Hussein, Islamic law was given a central role in the government in Iraq. Since 2014, ISIS has been imposing strict Sharia law on wider and wider swaths of the war-torn nation since America pulled its troops out. In Mosul, Iraq's second largest city, there were close to 60,000 Christians as recently as 2003.[87] Today, there are no known Christians in Mosul; they have all been either driven out or killed.[88]

* In Egypt, after a military coup ousted President Mohamed Morsi of the Muslim Brotherhood, Egyptian Muslims sought to take out their frustrations on Christians. According to CBS News:

> The ongoing political violence in Egypt has led to unprecedented attacks on the country's Coptic Christian minority, the worst in their history. Copts, who make up roughly 10 percent of the Egyptian population, were the target of revenge by Muslim mobs this summer.... Over 40 Christian churches all over Egypt were gutted by arson and looted— some over a thousand years old and full of priceless relics. Copts have also been murdered in ongoing sectarian violence.[89]

Indeed, many of the nations of the so-called "Arab Spring" whose revolutions were endorsed by President Obama have become deeply unstable, with growing violence—particularly against Christians. The "Arab Spring" has become the "Christian Winter" in the Middle East.

Treatment of Women

* In Amnesty International's most recent available report on Pakistan, which is fully governed by Sharia law, it is noted that:

> Women faced legal and de facto discrimination and violence at home and in public. The Aurat Foundation documented 8,539 cases of violence against women, including 1,575 murders, 827 rapes, 610 incidents of domestic violence, 705 honour killings and 44 acid attacks. In December, Pakistan's parliament sought to address this problem by passing the Acid Control and Acid Crime Prevention Bill 2010....[90]

In other words, disfiguring acid attacks against women became so common that Parliament had to pass a law limiting the availability of acid. Among the reasons for the disfiguring of acid attacks and honor killings of women are often a rejected marriage proposal or spurned sexual advances.

As a *Los Angeles Times* story on the phenomena noted:

> Awareness about the crime has improved... but Pakistan remains a patriarchal society where, particularly in rural areas, women's rights are routinely ignored. Many attacks go unreported, and even when victims lodge complaints, police and judges often halfheartedly pursue the cases.[91]

* In Saudi Arabia, a Sharia state, women cannot vote, drive, or go anywhere without a male chaperone.[92] If caught driving, they can face severe penalties including lashings.[93]

Amnesty International says:

> Women continued to face severe discrimination both in law and in practice. They must obtain the permission of a male guardian before they can travel, take paid work, engage in higher education or marry, and their evidence carries less weight in a court of law than that of men.[94]

In 2002, 15 girls died in a Saudi Arabian school fire because the "religious police" charged with upholding Sharia law would not let them leave the burning building—because they were not wearing the required robes and head coverings.[95]

* In Iran (not unique among Sharia-ruled nations), women are expected to adhere to the strict Sharia dress code, including wearing the *hijab* in public with no hair allowed to show. During crackdowns on "bad hijab," women have been detained, and even had court cases against them.[96] "Bad hijab" also resulted in a string of acid attacks on Iranian women in 2014.[97]

* In Nigeria, some areas are ruled by Sharia law, while others are not. The militant group Boko Haram, fighting to bring all of Nigeria under Sharia law, kidnapped more than 270 girls from

the Chibok boarding school in 2014. Most of them were said by the group to have been converted to Islam and married off to warriors.[98]

* As no less than *TIME Magazine* once noted, regarding the Muslim world:

> Women's rights are compromised further by a section in the Koran, Surah 4:34, that has been interpreted to say that men have "pre-eminence" over women or that they are "overseers" of women. The verse goes on to say that the husband of an insubordinate wife should first admonish her, then leave her to sleep alone and finally beat her. Wife beating is so prevalent in the Muslim world that social workers who assist battered women in Egypt, for example, spend much of their time trying to convince victims that their husbands' violent acts are unacceptable.[99]

International Relations

* The Pew survey of Muslim beliefs in 2013 contains a great deal of fascinating information. But it is perhaps even more fascinating to look at their 2005 survey of the Muslim world. Many of the questions did not make it to the 2013 survey, and it is not hard to see why. According to the 2005 poll:

> Anti-Jewish sentiment is endemic in the Muslim world....99% of Jordanians have a very unfavorable view of Jews. Large majorities of Moroccans, Indonesians, Pakistanis and six-in-ten Turks also view Jews unfavorably.[100]

Pew's 2013 poll asked Muslims questions about Muslim/Christian relations, but failed to ask any questions about Jews.

* In the enlightening 2005 poll, Muslims were asked how much confidence they had in Al Qaeda terror head Osama bin Laden, who at the time was still alive and on the run from U.S. and coalition forces. Sixty percent of Muslims in Jordan said they had "a lot/some" confidence in bin Laden. In Pakistan it was 51 percent. In Indonesia, 35 percent had at least some confidence in bin Laden—though as many as 58 percent did just two years earlier.

Keep in mind that those numbers represent more than 100 million people in the Muslim world who at some point after 9/11 expressed confidence in *Osama bin Laden*. That's a very hard number to square with the notion that the likes of bin Laden "hijacked" Islam and represent only a small, fringe movement.

The fact is, there is simply no Muslim-majority nation in the world in which Sharia law is practiced where freedom of speech or expression exists, where women have even basic rights, and where non-Muslims have freedom to peacefully practice other religions. Quite the contrary.

If "culture is religion externalized," then the picture painted of Islam by implementation of its purest forms in the Muslim world is a rather bleak one.

CHAPTER FOUR

FALSE EQUIVALENCE

It has become virtually axiomatic in the media and in the Obama Administration that all religions are more or less the same, and that all are equally guilty of misdeeds and violence. Indeed, it has become a matter of faith for many that Christianity, in the main, poses a threat of violence equal to Islam.

On ABC-TV's *The View*, co-hosts Rosie O'Donnell and Elizabeth Hasselbeck were discussing the American wars in Iraq and Afghanistan. O'Donnell sought to draw an equivalence between the Muslim terrorist's actions on 9/11 and the U.S. response to those actions, when this exchange took place:

O'DONNELL: As a result of the [9/11] attack and the killing of nearly 3,000 innocent people, we invaded two countries and killed innocent people in their countries.

HASSELBECK: But do you understand that, that the belief funding those attacks, okay, that is widespread. And if you take radical Islam and if you want to talk about what's going on there, you have to...

O'DONNELL: Wait just one second. *Radical Christianity is just as threatening as radical Islam* [loud applause] in a country like America where we have a separation of church and state. We're a democracy.[101]

Considering the information already presented in this book, such an assertion is astounding. In reality, nothing could be further from the truth. What O'Donnell is saying is literally nonsense. But she is by no means alone in her breathtaking assertion.

In recent years, in any public discussion of the dangers of radical Islam, it has become obligatory to insert the caveat that there is nothing particular to Islam that is encouraging violence, and that other religions (especially Christianity) are equally dangerous.

What is glaringly absent from most of these claims, however, is *evidence.* The trope is simply trotted out, everyone nods in agreement, and the issue is dispensed with.

In the rare cases where modern evidence is cited, it usually has to do with one particular issue: abortion clinic violence. Since it is occasionally raised—and is literally the only piece of supposed evidence from the past century that those drawing an equivalence between Islam and Christianity attempt to raise, it is worth looking at for a moment.

Fact: There have been eight total murders of abortion clinic doctors or employees in America, in six different incidents, at the hands of six different attackers. The first was in 1992; the most recent (as of this writing) was in 2009.

Additionally, the NARAL Pro-Choice America Foundation (a staunch abortion advocate) says that there have also been 17 attempted murders.[102] Most of these occurred in the same incidents as the previously mentioned killings.

Of the six killers, one, John Salvi, voiced some pro-Catholic sentiments but also "believed that the Freemasons, the Mafia and the Ku Klux Klan were conspiring to persecute Catholics."[103] Several psychiatrists at his trial testified that he was a paranoid schizophrenic,[104] and he later committed suicide in his prison cell.[105]

Another of the killers, Eric Robert Rudolph (who killed an abortion clinic security guard with a bomb, and was also responsible for the Olympic Park bombing in Atlanta at the 1996 Olympics) has repudiated Christianity—though there have been extensive attempts to connect him with it. In a letter written in prison, Rudolph said:

Many good people continue to send me money and books. Most of them have, of course, an agenda; mostly born-again Christians looking to save my soul. I suppose the assumption is made that because I'm in here I must be a 'sinner' in need of salvation, and they would be glad to sell me a ticket to heaven, hawking this salvation like peanuts at a ballgame. I do appreciate their charity, but I could really do without the condescension. They have been so nice I would hate to break it to them that I really prefer Nietzsche to the Bible.[106]

According to Rudolph's own words, he prefers the nihilism of Friedrich Nietzsche (who was best known for coining the phrase "God is dead," and wrote, among other books, *The Antichrist*, in which he poured out his disgust for Christianity) to the Bible, which all Christians believe to be the word of God.

So, if Salvi (who clearly had mental problems) and Rudolph (who has repudiated Christianity) are eliminated as being motivated by even a tangential relationship to Christianity, we are left with four abortion clinic killers with one degree or another Christian connections.

Four. In over two decades.

Agreeing that even one is too many, it is nevertheless instructive to compare that number with any *one day's* worth of news about jihadist attacks in the name of Islam. The notion that violence is more or less equally fueled by any interpretation of Christianity and any interpretation of Islam simply crumbles before the stark evidence.

Before going any further, it should be noted that virtually every Christian abhors and condemns abortion-doctor killings. Not only so, but they would immediately report it if they knew someone in their midst who was plotting such a thing to the authorities. These abortion clinic attacks were universally condemned by Christians when they occurred—and without hedging language implying that the victims themselves provoked the attacks.

Can the same be said of Islam? As we have noted before, it is true that the majority of Muslims in the world are against violence. Yet, as the 2013 Pew survey of Muslims showed, 28 percent of Muslims worldwide believe that suicide bombings and other forms of violence against civilians in defense of Islam are at least occasionally justified.[107] Using Pew's population numbers, which estimate that there were 1.62 billion Muslims in the world in 2010[108], we can estimate that there are over 450 million Muslims who refuse to unequivocally denounce violence in the name of Islam—more than the entire population of the United States and Mexico combined.

And yet, the media continues to lazily assert the false equivalence between violence in Christianity and violence in Islam.

Political Correctness Run Amok

One can almost see the wheels of equivalence turning in the heads of CBS News' veteran anchor Bob Schieffer and Republican Senator Lindsey Graham as they discussed the 2009 Fort Hood massacre on *Face the Nation*.

> SCHIEFFER: Do you think the fact that this man was a Muslim…uh, obviously he was either part of some terrorist plot—and I think most, uh, suggestions are that he wasn't. Uh, it's looking more and more like he was just, sort of, a religious nut. And you know Islam doesn't have a majority— or the Christian religion has its full, you know, full helping of nuts too. But do you think the fact that he was a Muslim may have caused the military to kind of step back and be reluctant to challenge him on this stuff, for fear that they'd be accused of discrimination or something like that?[109]

Schieffer's question is a legitimate one. But why the need to suddenly insert the red herring about Christians in the middle of it? As Schieffer bobs to-and-fro, hemming and hawing through a very important (and one would think obvious) question, it seems that he is at the very least deeply reluctant to ask it.

And Senator Graham is just as reluctant to straightly answer it.

GRAHAM: I hope not. I, uh, hope that's not the case, but to those members of the United States military who are Muslims, thank you for protecting our nation. Thank you for standing up against people who are trying to hijack your religion. I hope that's not the case, Bob, but we need… his actions do not reflect on…on…on the Islamic, Muslim faith any more than –

SCHIEFFER: Well I'm not suggesting they do –

GRAHAM: Any more than the burning cross –

SCHIEFFER: I'm not suggesting that.

GRAHAM: I know. But some people are. Some people are, and I want to say as a United States senator that I reject that.

This is a rather telling response to the extremely important question of whether the Army was precluded by political correctness from properly investigating Hasan before the shootings. Hasan was an increasingly radicalized Muslim who had expressed strong disagreement with the war in Iraq[110], was in email contact with terrorist imam Anwar al-Awlaki,[111] supported violent extremism in a class presentation[112], and shouted "Allahu akbar" as he mowed down his comrades.[113] Yet apropos of nothing, Schieffer and Graham fall all over each other to dismiss the question and assert that Christianity has its own problems. This is something less than a steely-eyed pursuit of the truth.

Truth Pushes Back

The militant atheist comedian Bill Maher has been no friend of Christianity, often ridiculing and mocking Christians on his television program and in his standup comedy. But reality can be a pesky thing, and the bloodshed wrought by radical Islam has begun intruding upon militant atheism's once-tidy view of "religion." In the wake of the deadly January, 2015 attack on the offices of the satirical newspaper *Charlie Hebdo* in Paris, Maher noted:

> I know most Muslim people would not have carried out an attack like this. But here's the important point. Hundreds of millions of them support an attack like this. They applaud an attack like this. What they say is, we don't approve of violence, but you know what, when you make fun of the prophet, all bets are off.[114]

On an appearance with Charlie Rose on PBS, they began to discuss ISIS's terrorism in Iraq. Rose once again tried to seek refuge in the media's false equivalence between Christianity and Islam—but Maher refused to let him get away with it. Their exchange is worth quoting at length:

> BILL MAHER: I saw Howard Dean on TV the other day and he said something along the order, he said the people in ISIS—he said "I'm about as Islamic as they are," you know, distancing the vast numbers of Islamic people around the world from them. That's just not true.
>
> CHARLIE ROSE: It is true.
>
> MAHER: It is not true, Charlie. There is a connecting tissue between –
>
> ROSE: Behind every Muslim is a future member of some radical?
>
> MAHER: Let me finish.
>
> ROSE: I was doing that.
>
> MAHER: There are illiberal beliefs that are held by vast numbers of Muslim people that –

ROSE: A vast number of Christians too.

MAHER: No, that's not true. Not true. Vast numbers of Christians do not believe that if you leave the Christian religion you should be killed for it. Vast numbers of Christians do not treat women as second class citizens. Vast numbers of Christians –

ROSE: I agree with that –

MAHER: – do not believe if you draw a picture of Jesus Christ you should get killed for it. So yes, does ISIS do Khmer Rouge-like activities where they just kill people indiscriminately who aren't just like them? Yes. And would most Muslim people in the world do that or condone that? No.

ROSE: No.

MAHER: But most Muslim people in the world do condone violence just for what you think.

ROSE: How do you know that?

MAHER: They do. First of all they say it. They shout it.

ROSE: Vast majorities of Muslims say that?

MAHER: Absolutely. There was a Pew poll in Egypt done a few years ago—82 percent said, I think, stoning is the appropriate punishment for adultery. Over 80 percent thought death was the appropriate punishment for leaving the Muslim religion. I'm sure you know these things.
ROSE: Well I do. But I don't believe –

MAHER: So to claim that this religion is like other religions is just naive and plain wrong. It is not like other religious. *The New York Times* pointed out in an op-ed a couple weeks ago that in Saudi Arabia just since August 4th, they think it was, they have beheaded 19 people. Most for non-violent crimes including homosexuality.[115]

Interestingly, Rose claims to be aware of the statistics that Maher is citing. Yet, in an act of stunning cognitive dissonance, he simultaneously (and steadfastly) insists that Christianity and Islam are equivalent.

Even biologist Richard Dawkins, perhaps the world's most outspoken atheist and critic of Christianity, recognizes that it is fallacious to claim any moral equivalence between Christianity and radical Islam. In the days following the jihad attack on *Charlie Hebdo* in Paris, Dawkins (who wrote the atheist screed *The God Delusion*) surprised many by posting on Twitter:

No, all religions are NOT equally violent. Some have never been violent, some gave it up centuries ago. One religion conspicuously didn't.[116]

If attempts to draw equivalence between Christianity and Islam were merely confined to the media, we might perhaps be able to overlook them. But when our government adopts the same mindset—and bases policy on it—there is reason for grave concern. Yet this is precisely what has happened.

The Prayer Breakfast Debacle

At the National Prayer Breakfast on February 5, 2015, just days after ISIS released a video to the world showing them immolating a Jordanian pilot in the name of Allah, President Obama addressed violence "so often perpetrated in the name of religion." He said:

Lest we get on our high horse and think this is unique to some other place, remember that during the Crusades and the Inquisition, people committed terrible deeds in the name of Christ. In our home country, slavery and Jim Crow all too often was justified in the name of Christ.

… And, first, we should start with some basic humility. I believe that the starting point of faith is some doubt—not being so full of yourself and so confident that you are right and that God speaks only to us, and doesn't speak to others, that God only cares about us and doesn't care about others, that somehow we alone are in possession of the truth.[117]

For weeks preceding the speech, Americans had been calling for President Obama to admit that acts of Islamic terrorism are, in fact, Islamic. He had steadfastly refused to do so despite overwhelming evidence.

It is interesting that, in the face of Islamic terrorism worldwide—in the same week in which Muslim radicals proudly displayed themselves incinerating a living human being, President Obama's instinct was to attack *Christians.* If one were concerned that President Obama does not understand the real issue—or that he is willfully ignorant about it—his speech at the National Prayer Breakfast would only show reasons for further concern.

While there have certainly been those who have done evil in Christ's name, President Obama also conveniently ignored that it was Christians who led the abolition movement, both in England and in America. Using Christ's name to justify slavery and racism is rightly denounced by virtually every Christian. Meanwhile, there still stands that Pew poll showing that as many as 28 percent of Muslims worldwide believe that suicide bombings that kill civilians in defense of Islam can at least occasionally be justified. While it was Christians who led us to abolition in America, can the president, as he engages in his cultural relativism, point to a similar example of Muslim-led social change that has brought freedom to generations of people?

In asserting the false equivalence between Christianity and Islam, it was odd—but typical—that the president then reached back a thousand years to the Crusades for another event with which to tarnish Christianity. When it comes to militant Islam, an internet search will usually show we only have to go back a few *minutes* to find outrageous violent atrocities.

But as the president employed this common rhetorical device for impugning Christianity, it is worth noting what the Crusades were actually about. Today, they are treated as a trump card, ending any argument in favor of Christianity by showing how supposedly bloodthirsty and imperialistic Christianity is capable of being (which is precisely the purpose for which President Obama invoked them). But historical ignorance abounds, and most today—including Christians, Muslims, and apparently American presidents—do not know much about them.

Far from being a baptized Christian quest to expand territory and enslave native peoples, the Crusades were, in fact, a reaction against previous Islamic aggression.

Thomas F. Maddon, Director of the Center for Medieval and Renaissance Studies at Saint Louis University (and one of the premier living scholars of the Crusades), writes:

> All the Crusades met the criteria of just wars. They came about in reaction [to] attacks against Christians or their Church. The First Crusade was called in 1095 in response to the recent Turkish conquest of Christian Asia Minor, as well as the much earlier Arab conquest of the Christian-held Holy Land. The second was called in response to the Muslim conquest of Edessa in 1144. The third was called in response to the Muslim conquest of Jerusalem and most other Christian lands in the Levant in 1187.
>
> In each case, the faithful went to war to defend Christians, to punish the attackers, and to right terrible wrongs.[118]

In other words, even the "smoking gun" evidence cultural relativists such as President Obama continually bring to the table to assail Christianity—which is a millennium old—is predicated on

Islam's historically-consistent war footing.

Author Jonah Goldberg, writing in the aftermath of the Presidential Prayer Breakfast speech, called President Obama to account for his assertions:

> [A]s odd as it may sound for a guy named Goldberg to point it out, the Inquisition and the Crusades aren't the indictments Obama thinks they are. For starters, the Crusades—despite their terrible organized cruelties—were a defensive war.[119]

Goldberg goes on to observe the often-overlooked fact that, while there were indefensible things that took place in the Inquisitions (especially in Spain), they were for the most part an *improvement* over the status quo in which local nobles were executing people without due process in order to satisfy mobs. Goldberg continues:

> But there's a very important point to make here that transcends the scoring of easy, albeit deserved, points against Obama's approach to Islamic extremism (which he will not call Islamic): Christianity, even in its most terrible days, even under the most corrupt popes, even during the most unjustifiable wars, was indisputably a force for the improvement of man.
>
> Christianity ended greater barbarisms under pagan Rome. The church often fell short of its ideals—which all human things do—but its ideals were indisputably a great advance for humanity. Similarly, while some rationalized slavery and Jim Crow in the U.S. by invoking Christianity, it was ultimately the ideals of Christianity itself that dealt the fatal blow to those institutions. Just read any biography of Martin Luther King Jr. if you don't believe me.[120]

In his thorough historical recounting of the beneficial formative effects of Christianity on life in the Western world, scholar Rodney

Stark pulls no punches with his readers:

> Christianity created Western Civilization. Had the followers
> of Jesus remained an obscure Jewish sect, most of you
> would not have learned to read and the rest of you would
> be reading from hand-copied scrolls. Without a theology
> committed to reason, progress, and moral equality, today
> the entire world would be about where non-European
> societies were in, say, 1800: a world with many astrologers
> and alchemists but no scientists. A world of despots, lacking
> universities, banks, factories, eyeglasses, chimneys, and
> pianos. A world where most infants do not live to the age
> of five and many women die in childbirth—a world truly
> living in "dark ages."

> The modern world arose only in Christian societies. Not
> in Islam. Not in Asia. Not in a "secular" society—there
> having been none. And all the modernization that has since
> occurred outside Christendom was imported from the
> West, often by colonizers and missionaries.[121]

As Stark observes, historically Christianity—and Christianity
alone—encouraged philosophical reflection and logical inference
from the premises contained in the text of the Bible, and believed
that such reflection could bring *progress*. "From the early days," Stark
notes, "Christian theologians have assumed that the application of
reason can yield an *increasingly accurate* understanding of God's
will."[122]

All anyone who wishes to maintain equivalence between
Christianity and Islam must do is take a good look at any society
deeply influenced by Christianity and then comparatively examine
any society deeply influenced by Islam—and if even a modicum of
honesty is involved, the illusion will immediately dissipate.

CHAPTER FIVE

WHY THEY DARE NOT CALL IT ISLAM

Separating Islam from those who commit terror in its name has been a longstanding goal of President Obama. In the first months of his presidency, speaking to an Egyptian audience at the University of Cairo, Obama said:

> I have known Islam on three continents before coming to the region where it was first revealed. That experience guides my conviction that partnership between America and Islam must be based on what Islam is, not what it isn't. And I consider it part of my responsibility as President of the United States to fight against negative stereotypes of Islam wherever they appear.[123]

From the outset of his presidency, Mr. Obama has outlined a program to disassociate "true Islam" (as he defines it) from those committing violence. He sees it as part of his responsibility as president, though of course no such responsibility is assigned to the president in America's Constitution.

Unfortunately, President Obama's caution does not extend itself to Christianity, where it appears he has been more than willing to resort to negative stereotypes, despite the fact that nearly 80 percent of the citizens of the nation he presides over identify themselves as Christians.[124] While being deeply concerned about his perception in the Muslim world, he shows little such concern about his perception in the Christian world.

At a fundraising event in liberal San Francisco in 2008, for instance, then-candidate Obama explained his view of the small-minded psychology of unemployed people in tiny towns in Pennsylvania and elsewhere:

> And it's not surprising then they get bitter, they cling to guns or religion or antipathy toward people who aren't like them or anti-immigrant sentiment or anti-trade sentiment as a way to explain their frustrations.[125]

For President Obama's speech on economics in 2009 at Georgetown University, a Catholic institution, the White House asked school officials to cover up an "IHS" monogram in the hall where the speech would take place.[126] "IHS" is a Greek abbreviation for the name of Jesus.

At the aforementioned National Prayer Breakfast in 2015, President Obama took the occasion of widespread national concern about the Islamic State in Iraq and Syria, who had just publicly murdered a Jordanian pilot, to attack *Christianity*.

Cultural Identification

In examining President Obama's communications, a pattern emerges. When speaking about Islam, he speaks in glowing terms about its purported positive influence on world history, its peace-loving people, and its supposed commitment to peace.

When speaking about Christianity on the other hand, despite his own self-professed Christianity, he speaks almost always in negative terms. "High horse," "Crusades," "slavery," "obscure,"— such phrases are quick to come from the president's tongue when he discusses Christianity.

Certainly there is nothing wrong with criticizing one's own

tradition. Sometimes such critiques are helpful and necessary. But when it comes to President Obama, the criticisms all flow in only one direction: toward Christianity. More than once, he's taken to ridiculing texts in the Bible.

Urging secularism in a keynote address at a conference called "Building a Covenant for a New America," Mr. Obama said:

> Which passages of Scripture should guide our public policy? Should we go with Leviticus, which suggests slavery is OK and that eating shellfish is abomination? How about Deuteronomy, which suggests stoning your child if he strays from the faith? Or should we just stick to the Sermon on the Mount—a passage that is so radical that it's doubtful that our own Defense Department would survive its application? So before we get carried away, let's read our Bibles. Folks haven't been reading their Bibles.[127]

In claiming that Jesus' Sermon on the Mount affirms same-sex partnerships (which President Obama was not willing to then call "marriages," though his stance later "evolved"), he dismissed the Apostle Paul, who wrote 13 of the New Testament's 27 books—by far the most of any New Testament author:

> I don't think it should be called marriage, but I think that it is a legal right that they should have that is recognized by the state. If people find that controversial, then I would just refer them to the Sermon on the Mount, which I think is, in my mind, for my faith, more central than an obscure passage in Romans.[128] *

---

* It should also be noted that, from a Christian perspective, President Obama is (at best) confused here. There is no contradiction between Jesus and Paul, though it is a mark of liberal theology to posit one. Historic Christianity is unified in believing that "All Scripture is breathed out [inspired] by God and profitable for teaching, for reproof, for correction, and for training in righteousness..." (1 Tim. 3:15, ESV, emphasis added). Jesus Himself said that Scripture "cannot be broken" (John 10:35). Thus, President Obama is far outside of the historic Christian mainstream, both in his interpretation of Scripture and his support for homosexual unions.

In the mind of the president, the first chapter of Paul's letter to the Romans, one of the key texts of the New Testament, is "obscure." A search for similar ridiculing of Islamic texts on the part of President Obama has yet to unearth any results.

Meanwhile, as President Obama maintains his near-constant criticisms of Christianity, he is fawning in his descriptions of Islam, often engaging in historical revisionism. As pressure mounted in early 2015 for Obama to simply say the obvious—that there is a religious motivation involved in Islamic terrorism—he seemed to double down on his position of solicitousness toward Islam. At a February 2015 summit countering "violent extremism" (with again no specific mention of *Islamic* extremism), Obama sought to stand in solidarity with Islam, claiming, "Here in America, Islam has been woven into the fabric of our country since its founding."[129]

This statement is wildly untrue. There was no significant wave of Muslim immigration to America until at least 1878, more than a century after the nation's founding.[130] Political commentator and author Ben Shapiro points out, there was a significant number of at least nominally Muslim slaves in early America, but Islam was viewed with great suspicion by the founders and the philosophers who influenced them.[131]

As historian Thomas S. Kidd notes:

> Benjamin Franklin's *Poor Richard* once wondered, "Is it worse to follow Mahomet [Muhammad] than the Devil?" For most early American observers, no such question was necessary: to follow the former meant following the latter.... In addition to using images of Islam for religious purposes, polemicists often used Islam and Muslim nations as the world's worst examples of tyranny and oppression, the very traits that the Revolutionaries meant to fight.[132]

In other words, while there have been *Muslims* in America since the start, *Islam* as a religion or a philosophy had no influence in America until well after the Civil War, and certainly was no part of the "fabric" of America at its founding.

While one can perhaps understand Obama's need (and the need of President Bush before him) to assure over a billion people that America is not at war with *all* of Islam, such statements inflating the role of Islam or bowdlerizing its true history have still been striking in their sheer untruthfulness.

However, none of this should be surprising for those who have been paying attention.

It is untrue and unfair to call President Obama a "secret Muslim" as some have done. He has publicly professed Christianity and refers to himself as a Christian. By definition, this essentially excludes him from being Muslim, since in Islam a *profession* of Islam is essential to the definition of being Muslim. There is really no room in Islamic theology for someone to be a Muslim while publicly and repeatedly professing to be a Christian.

To be fair, it is not only some conspiracy-minded Christians who have made this allegation. A liberal Egyptian newspaper, opposed to then-president Mohamed Morsi who ascended to power after the Obama administration removed its support from longtime president Hosni Mubarak, accused President Obama of being a full member of Morsi's Muslim Brotherhood organization. But no proof was ever forthcoming, and the allegation seemed to stem more from sour grapes than actual fact.[133]

As Robert Spencer, director of Jihad Watch (who has been otherwise highly critical of President Obama's handling of Islamic terrorism), points out:

> It is extremely unlikely that a Muslim would publicly proclaim himself a Christian over and over. While it is possible that this would be justified under Islam's doctrines of deception,* there is no evidence that Muslims have ever behaved this way. If Obama were a secret Muslim, he would be the first to carry out a sustained deception of claiming not to be a Muslim.[134]

---

* Spencer refers to the doctrines of *taqiyya* and *kitman*, which some Muslim sects have interpreted to mean lying about certain aspects of the faith (or telling half-truths) in the service of forwarding it.

But there is little doubt that, given his deference to the Muslim world, that Obama identifies with them in some fundamental way. Over and over again, his words and actions show that while he *professes* Christianity, he more personally *sympathizes* with Islam.

Speaking to a world audience at the United Nations General Assembly just two weeks after four Americans, including the U.S. Ambassador, were killed by Islamic terrorists in Libya, President Obama used the opportunity not to condemn Islamic terror as America mourned, but instead to condemn those who had allegedly mocked Muhammad in the YouTube video the administration was wrongly asserting had ignited the attacks.

In doing so, he virtually gave voice to the sentiments of radical Islamic terrorists. "The future must not belong to those who slander the prophet of Islam,"[135] said the President of the United States, lending credibility to those who would kill 13 at *Charlie Hebdo's* Paris offices a few years later because of "incendiary" cartoon drawings of Muhammad.

Recall that in his speech to the University of Cairo cited at the outset of this chapter, President Obama said, "I have known Islam on three continents before coming to the region where it was first revealed."[136]

The word "revealed" there is very—revealing.

In prepared remarks before a foreign audience, no words in a presidential speech are accidental. Muslims believe that Islam—via the Koran—was revealed directly by Allah to their prophet, Muhammad. By using the word "revealed" rather than saying something like "the region where it first originated," Obama was tacitly telling Muslims that he believed their religion comes from God.

Frank Gaffney, Jr. founder and president of the Center for Security Policy found the president's verbiage troubling:

An interesting choice of words that, "first revealed." Not "established," "founded" or "invented." The President is, after all, a careful writer, so he must have deliberately eschewed verbs that reflect man's role, in favor of the theological version of events promoted by Islam. Thus, Mr. Obama has gone beyond the kind of "respectful language" he has pledged to use towards Islam. He is employing what amounts to code—bespeaking the kind of submissive attitude Islam demands of all, believers and non-believers alike.[137]

Having spent many of his formative years as a child in Indonesian schools, Obama took Koran study classes there and has said of himself, "I was a little Jakarta street kid."[138]

Nicolas Kristoff of *The New York Times*, writing during Obama's first presidential campaign, said of an interview he conducted with then-candidate Obama:

Mr. Obama recalled the opening lines of the Arabic call to prayer, reciting them with a first-rate accent. In a remark that seemed delightfully uncalculated (it'll give Alabama voters heart attacks), Mr. Obama described the call to prayer as "one of the prettiest sounds on Earth at sunset."[139]

One of the lines of that call to prayer, recited in a "first-rate accent" by Mr. Obama to Kristoff, says, "I testify that Mohammad is the messenger of God."

By his own account, Christianity came to President Obama much later, after a non-religious upbringing, when he was in his mid-20's.[140] Working as a community organizer in Chicago, he began attending the church of controversial pastor Jeremiah Wright, where he says he committed his life to Christ.[141]

While it would be improper to question the sincerity of Obama's Christian faith (though he has not done much to help himself on that score when it comes to his obsequious statements about Islam), it would be fair to say is that he professes a liberal variety of the faith that differs widely from historic Christianity. It is a faith that does not posit an antithesis—or even a tension—between Islam and Christianity.

In an interview with religion writer Cathleen Falsani for the *Chicago Sun-Times* back in 2004 when he was an Illinois state senator running for the U.S. Senate, he said:

I'm rooted in the Christian tradition. I believe that there are many paths to the same place, and that is a belief that there is a higher power, a belief that we are connected as a people. That there are values that transcend race or culture, that move us forward, and there's an obligation for all of us individually as well as collectively to take responsibility to make those values lived.[142]

While this is a popular modern notion, it has little to do with the "Christian tradition." Historic Christianity is exclusive—as politically incorrect as that might be today. It holds that there is indeed one way to God. Furthermore, if Islam—which teaches that Muhammad said he was God's one, final, true prophet—is true, then Christianity must be false, and vice-versa since Jesus asserts that "no one comes to the Father but by me" (John 14:6). And the Apostle Peter repeated that claim, telling the religious authorities of his day, "…there is salvation in no one else, for there is no other name under heaven given among men by which we must be saved" (Acts 4:12).

Thus, while President Obama may be ecclesiastically Christian, his form of Christianity presents no significant barrier to his deference to and defense of Islam. On the contrary, he thinks it is a serious mistake for people to hold to any claims for the exclusive truth of Christianity.

Relativism

It was this very issue that President Obama addressed at the 2015 Prayer Breakfast. After equating Islam and Christianity (citing the Crusades from a thousand years ago), Obama went on to make this less controversial but more telling remark:

[F]irst, we should start with some basic humility. I believe that the starting point of faith is some doubt—not being so full of yourself and so confident that you are right and that God speaks only to us, and doesn't speak to others, that

God only cares about us and doesn't care about others, that somehow we alone are in possession of the truth.[143]

In that lengthy 2004 interview with the religion writer for the *Chicago Sun-Times*, he said much the same thing:

I'm a big believer in tolerance. I think that religion at its best comes with a big dose of doubt. I'm suspicious of too much certainty in the pursuit of understanding just because I think people are limited in their understanding.

I think that, particularly as somebody who's now in the public realm and is a student of what brings people together and what drives them apart, there's an enormous amount of damage done around the world in the name of religion and certainty.[144]

It should not surprise us that President Obama is unwilling to name the enemy when it comes to radical Islam. He has been saying the same thing publicly for more than a decade. Damage, he says, is not done in the name of a specific deity; it is done "in the name of religion and certainty." This is the president's worldview. It is a worldview he shares with many secular elites. And it is the worldview that drives his policies. This idea, that the cause of terrorism is "the inclination to see the world in black and white terms and believe that they alone possess the truth"[145] (as his Secretary of State John Kerry put it), is actually one of the drivers of President Obama's kid-glove handling of radical Islam.

Because the diagnosis is "certainty," the cure for what ails us is religious relativism—the notion that all religions are equally valid and true (or equally invalid and false). In President Obama's vision, the problem is not *what* people believe—the problem is belief itself, or at least too much of it. For him, beneficial religious faith is generic "higher power" faith—a faith which either does not believe much or cannot be much distinguished from any other kind of religious faith—while harmful religious faith believes strongly and distinctively. This is what lies at the heart of why he dares not call the terrorism Islam. For him, the problem is not Islam—it is deep conviction itself, regardless of the object.

And yet an analysis of the early followers of each religion shows that it is the *object* of faith that determines the trajectory of the religion, not the mere fervency of the faith itself. The early disciples of Muhammad followed their leader—who took them into war on the battlefield. Muhammad was a military leader who led conquests of Medina, Mecca, and Arabia.

Jesus' way was the way of self-sacrifice. When soldiers came to arrest him the night before his crucifixion, his disciple Peter drew a sword and cut off the ear of one of the captors. But rather than commending Peter, Jesus rebuked him, saying:

> Put your sword back into its place. For all who take the sword will perish by the sword. Do you think that I cannot appeal to my Father, and he will at once send me more than twelve legions of angels? But how then should the Scriptures be fulfilled, that it must be so? (Matthew 26:52-54).

Jesus then healed the soldier's ear, before being led off to his trial.

After Christ's death and resurrection, his followers were *certain* that he was the Messiah. In the immediate wake of Jesus' execution, they were fearful and hidden behind closed doors, but seeing him in his resurrected body transformed them. They began to boldly proclaim repentance, forgiveness of sins, and reconciliation to God, first in Jerusalem and ultimately to the whole world.

Contrast this with Muhammad and his first followers. Just one example:

> When Muhammad and his 3,000 Muslims in the Medina area in about A.D. 627 conquered the Banu Qurayza, a Jewish clan, and had taken about 2,000 prisoners, the women and children were separated from the men, leaving about 700 male prisoners (some sources say 800).

Muhammad ordered trenches be dug. The next day, five to six male prisoners at a time were brought to the trenches and forced to go to the edge, where his men then decapitated them. The slaughter began in the morning and ended with the last prisoner massacred by torchlight. Another time, Muhammad ordered one of his men to decapitate Kab ibn al-Ashraf (a half Jew from Medina), one of 80 accompanying assassinations. Then Kab's severed head was cast "at Mohammad's feet with the loud cry 'Allah is great,' and the Prophet heartily agreed.[146]

One group's certainty led them to offer the message of forgiveness and reconciliation to God. They were willing to suffer greatly in order to bring the Good News to those who had not yet heard. The other group's certainty led them to barbaric atrocities. *Certainty is not the problem here.* It is the *object* of one group's certainty that is the problem—namely the tenets and teachings of Islam—but this is something President Obama is unwilling to admit, for to do so is to admit that one faith may actually be superior to another.

There is no denying that there have been periods in history when Christians have acted inconsistently with the life and teachings of Jesus. And there are many Muslims throughout history—including the majority today—who have not strictly followed the life and teachings of Muhammad. Followers are not always faithful to the vision of the founder. But this cannot be overstated: Christians engaging in violence in the name of God are being inconsistent with their founder. Muslims who commit violence in the name of Allah are being *consistent* with their founder. A certainty of belief that Jesus is the Messiah leads one in a vastly different direction than does a certainty of belief that Muhammad is the true prophet of God.

Among the long-term results of certainty in Christianity have been freedom of religion, education for all (including women), care for the poor and sick (more hospitals in the world have been named for Christian religious figures than anything else), the flourishing of art and music, and constitutional government with separated powers, and a conviction that "blessed are the peacemakers."

As poet James Russell Lowell, who served as an American ambassador to England in the late 19th century, wrote:

> I challenge any skeptic to find a ten square mile spot on this planet where they can live their lives in peace and safety and decency, where womanhood is honored, where infancy and old age are revered, where they can educate their children, where the Gospel of Jesus Christ has not gone first to prepare the way.[147]

Empty Liberalism

President Obama proclaims religious certainty to be the enemy. Listening to Obama's prayer breakfast speech, the words of G.K. Chesterton, writing at the turn of the last century, ring as if he were sitting in the audience:

> [W]hat we suffer from today is humility in the wrong place. Modesty has moved from the organ of ambition. Modesty has settled upon the organ of conviction; where it was never meant to be. A man was meant to be doubtful about himself, but undoubting about the truth; this has been exactly reversed. Nowadays the part of a man that a man does assert is exactly the part he ought not to assert—himself. The part he doubts is exactly the part he ought not to doubt—the Divine Reason.…We are on the road to producing a race of men too mentally modest to believe in the multiplication table.[148]

It would be difficult to write a more accurate assessment of President Obama and the liberalism he espouses. While Mr. Obama counsels us to "humility" regarding the world-changing, culture-forming truths of Christianity (since in his view, religion appears to be an ethereal thing about which no one can actually know the truth), he seems absolutely certain in himself and his own inherent rightness.

Indeed, one will search in vain to find anyone who has ever characterized Barack Obama as "humble." Democratic Congressman Dennis Cardoza noticed this problem back in Obama's first term:

> Early in his administration, President/Professor Obama repeatedly referred to "teaching moments." He would admonish staff, members of Congress and the public, in speeches and in private, about what they could learn from him. Rather than the ideological or corrupt "I'm above the law" attitudes of some past administrations, President Obama projected an arrogant "I'm right, you're wrong" demeanor that alienated many potential allies.[149]

In describing the difficulty of President Obama's actual presidency compared with the promise so many held out upon his election, NBC's "Meet the Press" moderator Chuck Todd has written that:

> ...Obama's arrogance got the better of him. And at the end of the day, arrogance may be a better descriptor than naïveté.[150]

How many times has the American public heard the president insist (with great certainty) that he was on "the right side of history" while undertaking yet another action to overturn thousands of years of civilization?

President Obama counsels no "humility" when it comes to uprooting marriage—the fundamental societal institution for all of human history. He shows no "humility" when it comes to establishing (in Obamacare) one of the largest, most costly government programs in history—against the stated will of the majority of the people. He shows no "humility" when it comes to upturning millennia of Western ethical thought by asserting that women have a "right" to kill their children in the womb at any stage of development.

Indeed, American liberals are quite certain that they have a corner on the truth when they argue with certitude that the transgendered, bi-sexual linebacker should be able to use the women's restroom. They are quite certain that they can read the thoughts of those who disagree with them as they impute to their opponents deep-seated racism or sexism or acts of "micro-aggression," and even work toward criminalizing inward thoughts under the guise of "hate crime" laws.

The only things they are not certain about are those things of actual, fundamental importance—the kinds of things upon which a thriving society is built. And they see this uncertainty as a virtue.

This "modest" liberalism, which lacks conviction on the greatest questions mankind faces, while pressing with great certitude for no higher purpose than unbridled sexual behavior, has insufficient resources to deal with a threat like militant Islam. This secular relativism, so prominent in Europe, is oxygen to the fire of radical Islam. While European liberals thoughtfully rub their chins in uncertainty, Islam consumes more and more of their continent and acts of Muslim violence increase by the year. And many are increasingly concerned the same thing will happen here in the face of Obama's relativism.

The answer is not to cultivate uncertainty—which is a fool's errand. Such a bankrupt agenda collapses in on itself; should we be certain that basic uncertainty is the answer, for instance?

The answer is to cultivate certainty in the *truth*. From a Christian standpoint, there is no virtue in doubting truth. It is the furthest thing from humble to ignore the Word of God. Just as a child pretending not to hear his parents' instruction is not "humble," neither is ignoring what God has said.

"I am the way, and the truth, and the life. No one comes to the Father except through me," said Jesus (John 14:6).

Is President Obama being "humble" by saying that Jesus was wrong?

Indeed, it was Pontius Pilate, in the act of turning Jesus over for crucifixion, who sounds the cry of the modern liberal:

Jesus answered, "You say that I am a king. For this purpose I was born and for this purpose I have come into the world—to bear witness to the truth. Everyone who is of the truth listens to my voice."

Pilate said to him, "What is truth?" (John 18:37b-38).

And in a similar vein, standing before the attendees of the National Prayer Breakfast, President Obama informs the nation that "the starting point of faith is some doubt, " and counsels us to give up certainty in the truth.

In actuality, this is nothing less than a prescription for cultural suicide. Liberalism's hand-wringing doubts and "humility" on matters of basic truth present no barrier whatsoever to the rapid spread of radical Islam.

What *does* present a barrier is adherence to real truth—rich, fibrous, steely *truth*. It is certainty in the truth that will set us free. It is truth—Christian truth—which guarantees our liberties and provides a solid structure for a tolerant society.

As Christian pastor John Piper has written:

Christians are tolerant of other faiths not because there is no absolute truth or that all faiths are equally valuable, but because the one who is Absolute Truth, Jesus Christ, forbids the spread of his truth by the sword. Christian tolerance is the commitment that keeps lovers of competing faiths from killing each other. Christian tolerance is the principle that puts freedom above forced conversion, because it's rooted in the conviction that forced conversion is no conversion at all. Freedom to preach, to teach, to publish, to assemble for worship—these convictions flow from the essence of the Christian faith. Therefore we protect it for all.[151]

Names and Labels

There is a great deal at stake in President Obama's refusal to refer to negative attributes of Islam as "Islamic." As noted, his refusal stems from his particular worldview, and even though *naming the problem* is a primary step in solving any problem, this is, in and of itself, a near-revolutionary act in our postmodern, relativistic age.

Indeed, affixing labels to behavior once considered deviant, or identifying certain beliefs as unacceptable is considered one of the greater crimes that can be committed in today's "tolerant" society. What cannot be tolerated is affixing a label to a person or group that would denote disapproval or lack of acceptance of them. Whether the issue is gender, religion, or politics, labeling is "offensive" and to be avoided at all costs. Since identity is supposedly fluid (witness the ever-growing alphabet soup of acronyms propounded by those in the homosexual movement who say gender identity is an amorphous, shape-shifting, mutable thing), labels unnecessarily restrict and confine, and are, we are told, just the reflection of "socially constructed reality," not of reality itself.

This failure to name or label has its roots in postmodern cultural and epistemological relativism, which claims there is no overarching standard by which one culture or its values can be judged against another. As a result, it is claimed, we must insist that all cultures and all values (including religious values) are equally valid and equally good.

From a biblical standpoint, this perspective utterly fails.

In the Garden of Eden, God gave Adam, the first man, the task of naming each of the animals in creation (Genesis 2:19-20). As Christian theologians have noted, this naming process was one of the first acts of Adam's obedience to God's command that he take dominion over the creation.

In reality, naming things is simply a very basic mark of rationality and sensibility. At the most basic level, words are an important part of how we distinguish one thing from another. We cannot have a society, or even so much as an intelligible conversation, without using words to make distinctions. The entire purpose of words, the entire purpose of *communicating*, is to accurately distinguish something from something else in some way. Every sentence, every statement, is an attempt to communicate some state of affairs—as opposed to all of the other possible states of affairs.

A statement as simple as "I'm going to the grocery store" is rife with "labels." It communicates things about who is taking action (namely: me), what sort of action is being taken (I'm leaving my present location and going somewhere else), the kind of place I'm headed to (a market with food and other items daily-need items).

There is no point in having a discussion—or even speaking—unless you are distinguishing among things. Words are labels, and without them, communication becomes meaningless noise. (And indeed, this is essentially what many postmodern theorists, like the late French philosopher Jacques Derrida, more or less claim. They do not seem to grasp the irony of writing books that tell people communication is meaningless).

Making distinctions is the difference between life and death. If we cannot distinguish the label for the salt from the label for the rat poison we die. When the avant-garde composer John Cage began incorporating "chance" into his music (random events that could not be repeated or replicated, as a statement on the meaninglessness of musical patterns), Christian philosopher Francis Schaeffer noted that Cage did not employ the same philosophy of meaninglessness to his hobby of collecting mushrooms for cooking. Such an application would have quickly led to death by poisoning.

This is no mere academic problem. In another context, author Robert J. Reilly, who is a former Senior Advisor for Information Strategy for the Secretary of Defense, noted:

> Misnaming things necessarily leads to moral and political disorder.... Without the right word, one will not only get the relationship of things wrong, but what something actually is will be wrong, as well. The corruption of language spells the termination of justice, for it prevents us from knowing what things are, or how properly to speak of them, or to use rather than abuse them—just as when a black man was called a piece of property and used as an "article of merchandise," rather than a human being.[152]

Labels matter. A culture that rejects labels rejects truth. And a culture that rejects truth embraces death.

Lest anyone think applying this analysis to President Obama's thought infers too much, let us not forget that he has come right out and stated it—in unvarnished terms. In his book written for the 2008 presidential campaign, *The Audacity of Hope*, Obama says:

> Implicit in [the U.S. Constitution's] structure, in the very idea of ordered liberty, was a rejection of absolute truth, the infallibility of any idea or ideology or theology or "ism," any tyrannical consistency that might lock future generations into a single, unalterable course...."[153]

Reilly aptly characterizes Obama's remarks:

> In other words, truth leads to tyranny. Truth does not set you free; it imprisons. Moral relativism sets you free. Then you can do what you want. But it is absurd for Obama to say that the Founders of the United States did not believe in absolute truths. Had this been so, there would have been no Declaration of Independence ("We hold these truths...") and no Constitution. Obama is reading his own moral relativism back into the document and then trying to use it to legitimize the very opposite of what it proclaims.[154]

Contrary to President Obama's assertions, ordered liberty is *impossible* without certain "self-evident truths" as the framers of the Declaration called them. A written Constitution whose meaning can be arbitrarily changed by any judge or politician on a whim is no constitution at all. While the framers certainly allowed for future generations to modify the founding documents, they could only do so through a process, which again is fundamental to ordered liberty. Room was left for society to learn new things and adjust, but it was always to be within the framework provided by absolute truth. Without the pillars of absolute, self-evident truth driven into the ground, all that would be left is a flimsy, pliant structure that is easily torn down—precisely what the founders were seeking to avoid, and which President Obama seems to embrace.

This is not to say, of course, that President Obama has embraced every aspect of the utter meaninglessness of postmodern relativism. But these are strong currents in our culture, and the currents are even stronger at our elite, liberal institutions like Harvard Law School, where the president received his law degree. After spending his childhood abroad, Barack Obama was influenced by those on the far left, including communist party member Frank Marshall Davis, and avowed Marxist William Ayers, both of whom openly reject any notion that anything good could be attributed to either America or to historic Christianity. The president's philosophical bent toward cultural and religious relativism, nurtured and cultivated by his schooling and his mentors, is now finding expression in his policies and decisions.

We all have a worldview—a set of spectacles through which we view and interpret the world. Like with actual spectacles, they and their effect on what we see often go unnoticed. And so it is with Barack Obama. He is the President of the United States and a professing Christian. Yet his spectacles—his worldview—causes him to reflexively identify with those who see America and Christianity as negative forces. As a politician, he is obligated to tip his cap toward America and Christianity, yet it never seems like he is entirely comfortable doing so. His reflex, as evidenced at the National Prayer Breakfast and in his University of Cairo speech, is to tip his cap toward Islam and Muslim society.

CHAPTER SIX

THE REAL CURE

Naming the problem is essential, but we must not stop there. That is only the first step, not a solution in itself. The solution is not to abandon the truth as the majority in Europe have done, thus creating a vacuum that is rapidly being filled by a radical Islamist takeover of culture and society.

Solutions are not easy to come by. America and a number of nations have led a "war on terror" since 2002, which, while suppressing some cells of Islamic terrorists, has allowed others to crop up—some more violent and dangerous than those that preceded them. Part of the problem in this case, too, has been a failure (beginning with the George W. Bush administration) to name the actual enemy, as if one could go to war against "terror"—which is a tactic—rather than against a defined group of people. Haziness in the mission has led to haziness in the result. And even when the brave American military has won decisive battles, later political maneuvering has often turned their victories to ashes.

America and other western nations will have to decide both strategically and politically what the best course of physical action is against this new round of Islamic terrorism. But as we have seen, such "solutions" are usually provisional at best, and at worst they can unleash the law of unintended consequences. Now, after more than 6,000 American men and women have given their lives in Afghanistan and Iraq battling terrorists since 2002, we see Iraq,

Afghanistan, Libya, Syria, and numerous other nations sinking to new levels of violence and terroristic activity. The situation for Christians in Iraq has become far worse than it ever was under Saddam Hussein.

If further military action against the likes of ISIS and Boko Haram is undertaken, it is now clear that even if such action is necessary, it will not be sufficient.

At root this is a clash of ideas and core beliefs. The *ultimate* solution can only come if this fact is recognized.

The Gospel

The Gospel of Jesus Christ turns the violence of Islam on its head. In Islam, people die for their god. In Christianity, God came as a human being and dies for his people. From this truth has sprung the magnificent cultural inheritance of Western civilization— while Islamic societies have largely remained at a standstill as the scientific and cultural advances of the West passed them by. Yet political correctness often keeps us from stating the obvious. Can President Obama, as he pronounces "a pox on all their houses" and shudders at the notion that all religions might *not* be the same, point to a single Muslim-dominated society that has produced political, economic, and religious freedom? Or that has elevated the place of women in society? Or that has brought sustained security and prosperity to the average citizen?

In Muslim theology, the Christian, biblical concept of the Trinity is rejected in favor of the radical, undifferentiated oneness of God. In Christian Trinitarian theology, relationship is inherent to the nature of God. The Father, the Son, and the Holy Spirit are in perfect communion with one another—one in nature but three in person—even before creation. Thus, God is and always has been a loving, relational God—throughout all eternity.

The Islamic conception, which incorrectly sees Christianity as polytheistic (meaning: having more than one God), instead asserts the radical oneness of God. Thus, God (or "Allah") has no inherent capability for relationship. Relationship with anything "other" is only something that comes after creation, but is incidental to Allah's eternal character.

Because of this radical oneness, many scholars have pointed out that Muslims find God virtually unapproachable. Without a concept of relationship with God as in Christianity, there is no assurance of Heaven except through martyrdom.

In the words of Stephen Masood, who came from a sectarian Muslim background in Pakistan and now operates a Christian outreach called Jesus to Muslims:

> [Islamic terrorists] believe that, well, if we are killed, we will go straight into Paradise. It's much easier for us to go into Paradise that way than to performing all the ritual performance and everything and still not knowing that we are going to Paradise of God or not. But because the Koran says that martyrs killed in the way of God, or in the fight for God, they will go straight into the Paradise of God.[155]

As many have recognized, mankind is incurably religious. We are created for worship and for fellowship with God. And lacking access to God, we are liable to invent ways to try to reach him (or replace him) on our own—many of which will be destructive. Thus, the proper Christian response to Islam is not fear, but love and compassion. In this case, as in so many others, Jesus himself sets the pattern for us. First, there is his well-known Great Commission, in which we are instructed to:

> Go therefore and make disciples of all nations, baptizing them in the name of the Father and of the Son and of the Holy Spirit, teaching them to observe all that I have commanded you (Matthew 28:19-20).

We also have the striking story recorded in John 4 of the Samaritan woman Jesus meets at the well. There are daunting cultural barriers separating Jesus and the woman. First is the fact that she is a woman. In Jesus' first century Jewish context, casually talking with a woman would have been highly unusual. Beyond that, she was a Samaritan—a member of the group most at odds with Jesus' fellow Jews. John sums it up succinctly in his account of the meeting, writing in John 4:9:

> The Samaritan woman said to him, "How is it that you, a Jew, ask for a drink from me, a woman of Samaria?" (For Jews have no dealings with Samaritans.)

It seems that many Jewish people considered being Samaritan to be equal to demon-possession, at one point asking Jesus himself, "Are we not right in saying that you are a Samaritan and have a demon?" (John 8:48).

While his disciples "marveled that he was talking with a woman" (John 4:27), Jesus crossed the cultural divide in order to share the Good News of his kingdom with the woman. He opens the kingdom to those who seem most opposed to his followers, and invites them to be forgiven, cleansed, and transformed.

Indeed, the Bible is clear that all of us start out alienated from God. "For all have sinned and fall short of the glory of God" it tells us (Romans 3:23) —from the pen of the former Saul of Tarsus, who delighted in persecuting Christians and breathed out murderous threats against them (Acts 9:1), until his own encounter with the risen Christ transformed him into the man we now know as the Apostle Paul, arguably history's greatest and most important Christian evangelist.

Nobody is beyond the grace of God—even those who think they are doing a service to God by killing Christians (John 16:2). It is easy to see such people as the "other"—as the enemy to be avoided at all costs. While we do not solve this problem by pretending Islam is something it is not, or that terrorism is not a sizable factor among certain segments of Muslims, we also do not solve it via the erroneous ditches on either side of the road: avoidance on the one side, or counter-violence on the other side.

It is within the purview of the government, which has been specifically ordained by God to protect and defend the people by taking up arms against evildoers ("the sword" in Romans 13:4), to strategically decide when, where, and how Islamic violence must be met by counter-violence. But as Christians—as the church— our primary role must be the same as Christ's: "to seek and save the lost" (Luke 19:10). Military campaigns can sometimes stop the immediate threat, but a long-term solution requires cultural change. And a cultural change will require a *religious* change.

In the multicultural, politically correct world of President Obama and the Left, such a statement is considered dangerously radical. It says a great deal about this struggle between worldviews that the desire to see people come to salvation and a culture be transformed from barbarism is considered "dangerously radical," while they cannot bring themselves to say the same of the Islamic ideology that drives the onslaught of terrorism around the world.

Transformation

As a result of the tireless, often dangerous work of Christian missionaries in the Muslim world, the Gospel of Jesus Christ is beginning to change hearts there. Faisal Malick, for instance, was a Sunni Muslim born in Pakistan. He was a lifelong believer in the tenets of Islam until something drastically changed him in 1994, when, like so many other Muslims who have come to trust in Jesus, he believes he heard the audible voice of Jesus himself.

> I had an encounter with God and his presence went right through me, went right around me, and I heard an audible voice in response to my question, "God, what are you doing here? I thought these Christians are the bad guys." And he said, "No, these are my children." He said it three times. And it was like a veil came off my eyes and I knew that Jesus is the Son of God.[156]

For many years, it seemed to Christians that the Muslim world was virtually impenetrable. But as Malick explains:

[T]oday what we're hearing about is there's literally millions of Muslims coming to Christ all around the world. And they're having dreams and visions of Jesus literally. Forty percent of the Muslim people that come to Christ around the world today, come as a result of a dream or a vision. Something really exciting is happening and something has changed on the course of the world, and I believe it's a very unique time where God is reaching out to the Muslim world. I believe it's their season.[157]

As the late Dr. D. James Kennedy noted on the first anniversary of the 9/11 attacks:

Muhammad said that people were to give their sons for Allah. The Bible says that God gave His Son for you and me. Those are as diametrically different as they possibly could be.

Christ said, *"Thou shalt love the Lord thy God with all thy heart, and with all thy soul, and with all thy mind. This is the first and great commandment. And the second is like unto it, Thou shalt love thy neighbor as thyself"* (Matthew 22:37-39, KJV)—not to engage in Jihad, not to kill them, but rather, to love them. We are told that we are to love not only our neighbors, but we are to love even our enemies….We are to present the news to them that the Son of God died, even for mass murderers, and that He is willing to forgive them and cleanse them and indeed, take them to Paradise—not earned by shedding other men's blood, but earned by the Son of God shedding His own blood for us.[158]

The Blindness Continues

On February 15, 2015, ISIS released a video of 21 Egyptian Coptic Christians being lined up on their knees and beheaded. The video was titled, "A Message Signed With Blood to the Nation of the Cross."[159] The caption accompanying the video denoted the victims as "The people of the cross, followers of the hostile Egyptian church."[160]

In its statement denouncing the killings, the Obama Administration could not bring itself to call the victims "Christians," despite the fact that ISIS clearly stated that the killings targeted Christians and were a message to Christians. Doing so would force them to admit that, far from random, these attacks have a specific religious motivation stemming from a well-established religious position.

Instead, the administration noted "the despicable and cowardly murder of twenty-one Egyptian *citizens*..." and made sure to again remark that ISIS "is unconstrained by faith, sect, or ethnicity."[161]

Yet just days before, when an atheist shot and killed three Muslim students in what police said was a dispute about a parking space in North Carolina, President Obama made the Islamic faith of the victims an issue despite the fact that no immediate evidence pointed to it as a motive, saying, "No one in the United States of America should ever be targeted because of who they are, what they look like, or how they worship."[162]

It is a strange, troubling blindness that has befallen the American government and media. As Christians—as people of the truth—we must not participate in that blindness. Instead, we plead with the Lord to remove that blindness. And even if healing is not forthcoming, we stand as Shadrach, Meshach, and Abednego, who said to the Babylonian king:

> ...[O]ur God whom we serve is able to deliver us from the burning fiery furnace, and he will deliver us out of your hand, O king. But if not, be it known to you, O king, that we will not serve your gods or worship the golden image that you have set up (Daniel 3:17-18).

Whatever the results, we cannot bow to the idol of the prevailing relativism and political correctness that guides the president. We cannot give up the truth.

Instead, with eyes wide open and clad in the full armor of God, we must call upon the state to do its proper job of protecting the nation, while we do the work of going—and sending others—to share the transformative Good News of the Heavenly Father who sent his only Son into the world so that we can have true, lasting peace with God and with one another.

War and Peace

Just days after the 21 Coptic Christians were murdered by ISIS in Libya, Beshir Kamel, the brother of Bishoy Estafanos Kamel and Samuel Estafanos Kamel, who were both among the killed, was interviewed on SAT 7, a Christian network beaming into the Middle East. The host, Maher Fayez, asked Beshir a radical question. Here was their exchange (which the network translated from the Arabic):

Q. I want to ask you a question on your faith.

BESHIR: Go ahead please.

Q. Would you get upset or someone from your family get upset if we ask for forgiveness to those who killed your brothers?

BESHIR: Forgiveness to whom?

Q. For those who slayed and killed.

BESHIR: Today I was having a chat with my mother....I asked her, "What will you do if you see those ISIS members passing on the street and I told you 'that's the man who slayed your son?'" She said, "I will ask God to open his eyes and ask him in our house, because he helped us enter the Kingdom of God."

Q. Dear, with this good spirit, I ask you to pray for them... ISIS members, now that you are on the air.

BESHIR: [praying] Dear God, please open their eyes to be saved. And to quit their ignorance and the wrong teachings they were taught.

Q. Amen, my dear, amen.[163]

The labels matter. It was Christians who were attacked *because they were Christians* by Muslims *acting in the name of Islam.* Yet a Christian family who lost sons to the savagery of radical Islam does not seek revenge. Instead, they pray for the salvation of the attackers. One faith leads in one direction; the other faith leads in the opposite direction. Nothing could more powerfully demonstrate the true difference between Christianity and radical Islam.

ENDNOTES

1 "'ISIS' vs. 'ISIL' vs. 'Islamic State': The political importance of a much-debated acronym," Jaime Fuller, *Washington Post*, September 9, 2014. http://www.washingtonpost.com/blogs/the-fix/wp/2014/09/09/isis-vs-isil-vs-islamic-state-the-political-importance-of-a-much-debated-acronym/

2 "Militants outline chilling five-year plan for global domination," John Hall, *DailyMail.com*, June 30, 2014. http://www.dailymail.co.uk/news/article-2674736/ISIS-militants-declare-formation-caliphate-Syria-Iraq-demand-Muslims-world-swear-allegiance.html#ixzz3QnS4Mzrs

3 "French Soldiers Guarding Jewish Site Are Attacked," Maïa de La Baume and Dan Bilefsky, *NYTimes.com*, http://www.nytimes.com/2015/02/04/world/europe/charlie-hebdo-sets-date-for-next-issue.html?_r=0

4 "New allegations of Saudi involvement in 9/11," Jim Sciutto and Laura Koran, CNN.com, February 4, 2015. http://www.cnn.com/2015/02/03/politics/9-11-attacks-saudi-arabia-involvement/index.html

5 "17 soldiers killed in Boko Haram attacks in Cameroon" Indo-Asian News Service via *Daijiworld.com*, February 4, 2015. http://www.daijiworld.com/news/news_disp.asp?n_id=294811

6 "At least 32 killed in Egypt as militants attack army and police targets in Sinai," Patrick Kingsley, *TheGuradian.com*, January 30, 2015. http://www.theguardian.com/world/2015/jan/29/egypt-army-police-sinai-el-arish-sheikh-zuwayed-rafah

7 "Suicide bomber hits Afghan funeral," *BBC.com*, January 29, 2015. http://www.bbc.com/news/world-asia-31041820

8 "Explosion Kills Dozens at Shiite Mosque in Pakistan," Saba Imtiaz, *New York Times*, January 31, 2015. http://www.nytimes.com/2015/01/31/world/asia/blast-kills-scores-at-mosque-in-southern-pakistan.html

9 "Islamic State not Islamic? Kerry, Obama questioned over ISIS claims," *FoxNews.com*, September 18, 2014. http://www.foxnews.com/politics/2014/09/18/islamic-state-not-islamic-kerry-obama-questioned-over-isis-claims/

10 "Four men charged with helping deli terrorist," Peter Allen,
    DailyMail.com, January 21, 2015. http://www.dailymail.co.uk/news/
    article-2919696/Four-men-charged-helping-deli-terrorist-Amedy-
    Coulibaly-supplying-weapons-Paris.html

11 "Obama: The Vox Conversation," Matthew Yglesias, Vox.com,
    February 9, 2015. http://www.vox.com/a/barack-obama-interview-vox-
    conversation/obama-foreign-policy-transcript

12 "Real Time with Bill Maher," HBO, October 3, 2014 via video at *Real
    Clear Politics*, http://www.realclearpolitics.com/video/2014/10/03/bill_
    maher_vs_ben_affleck_on_islam_mafia_that_will_[ExpletiveDeleted]_
    kill_you_if_you_say_the_wrong_thing.html

13 "Ben Affleck: Sam Harris and Bill Maher 'racist' and 'gross' in views
    of Islam," Ben Child, *The Guardian*, October 7, 2014. http://www.
    theguardian.com/film/2014/oct/06/ben-affleck-bill-maher-sam-harris-
    islam-racist

14 "Bill Maher vs. Ben Affleck On Islam: "Mafia That Will [Expletive] Kill
    You If You Say The Wrong Thing" *Real Clear Politics*, October 3, 2014.
    http://www.realclearpolitics.com/video/2014/10/03/bill_maher_vs_
    ben_affleck_on_islam_mafia_that_will_[ExpletiveDeleted]_kill_you_if_
    you_say_the_wrong_thing.html

15 "The World's Muslims: Religion, Politics, and Society," Pew Research,
    "Chapter 1: Beliefs About Sharia," April 30, 2013. http://www.pewforum.
    org/2013/04/30/the-worlds-muslims-religion-politics-society-beliefs-
    about-sharia/#how-should-sharia-be-applied

16 Ibid.

17 "CBS Defends Ben Affleck Following Battle With Bill Maher Over
    Radical Islam, Jeffrey Meyer, *NewsBusters.org* October 6, 2014. http://
    newsbusters.org/blogs/jeffrey-meyer/2014/10/06/cbs-defends-ben-
    affleck-following-battle-bill-maher-over-radical#sthash.TleGQvzl.dpuf

18 "Why Ben Affleck Is Right, Bill Maher Is Wrong, And Sam Harris Is
    Jaded About Islam," H.A. Goodman, *The Huffington Post*, October 6,
    2014. http://www.huffingtonpost.com/h-a-goodman/why-ben-affleck-
    is-right_b_5938270.html

19 "Bill Maher's Dangerous Critique of Islam," Peter Beinart, *The
    Atlantic*, October 9, 2014. http://www.theatlantic.com/international/
    archive/2014/10/bill-maher-dangerous-critique-of-islam-ben-
    affleck/381266/

20 "Petition All You Want, Bill Maher Will Speak at Berkeley," Sally
    Kohn, *Vanity Fair*, December 2014. http://www.vanityfair.com/news/
    politics/2014/12/bill-maher-interview-islam-berkeley

21 "Furious Ben Affleck blasts Bill Maher and guests," Wills Robinson,
    Daily Mail UK, October 4, 2014. http://www.dailymail.co.uk/news/

article-2780960/It-s-gross-s-racist-Ben-Affleck-clashes-guest-Bill-Maher-talk-claims-Islam-motherload-bad-ideas-host-compares-religion-Mafia.html#ixzz3S1t1LMNu Follow us: @MailOnline on Twitter | DailyMail on Facebook

22 "Ben Affleck in passionate defence of Islam on Bill Maher show," Harriet Alexander, *The Telegraph*, October 5, 2014. http://www.telegraph. co.uk/news/worldnews/northamerica/usa/11141733/Ben-Affleck-in-passionate-defence-of-Islam-on-Bill-Maher-show.html

23 "Sniper suspect John Allen Muhammad's meltdown," Alex Tizon, *Seattle Times*, November 10, 2002. http://community.seattletimes.nwsource. com/archive/?date=20021110&slug=killer103

24 "Snipers an 'Army Veteran' & 'Jamaican Teenager' — 10/25/2002 CyberAlert," Brent Baker, Media Research Center, October 25, 2002. http://www.mrc.org/biasalerts/snipers-army-veteran-jamaican-teenager-10252002-cyberalert#1

25 "Mother of Lee Malvo: 'Save His Life,'" Jeffrey Kofman, *ABC News*, November 10, 2003. http://abcnews.go.com/GMA/story?id=128209

26 "Malvo sketches depicted 'jihad," Andrea F. Siegel, *Baltimore Sun*, December 4, 2003. http://www.baltimoresun.com/news/maryland/bal-te.md.malvo04dec04-story.html#page=1

27 "Malvo drawings depict Jihad, failure," Serge F. Kovalevski, *Washington Post*, December 3, 2003. Accessed at: http://articles.chicagotribune. com/2003-12-07/news/0312070371_1_lee-boyd-malvo-john-allen-muhammad-sniper

28 "Hasan's e-mail exchange with al-Awlaki; Islam, money and matchmaking," Larry Shaughnessy, July 20, 2012, http://security.blogs. cnn.com/2012/07/20/hasans-e-mail-exchange-with-al-awlaki-islam-money-and-matchmaking/

29 "Hasan's Therapy: Could 'Secondary Trauma' Have Driven Him to Shooting?" Tim McGirk, *TIME.com*, November 7, 2009, http://content. time.com/time/nation/article/0,8599,1936407,00.html

30 "CBS Features NY Mayor Bloomberg Speculating Bomber Was Mad About ObamaCare," Brent Baker, *NewsBusters.org*, May 3, 2010. http:// newsbusters.org/blogs/brent-baker/2010/05/03/cbs-features-ny-mayor-bloomberg-speculating-bomber-was-mad-about-obamac#sthash. HoibyGiA.dpuf

31 "Sources: Shahzad Had Contact With Awlaki, Taliban Chief, and Mumbai Massacre Mastermind." Richard Esposito and Chris Vlasto, and Chris Cuomo, *ABC News*, May 6, 2010. http://abcnews.go.com/ Blotter/faisal-shahzad-contact-awlaki-taliban-mumbai-massacre-mastermind/story?id=10575061

32 "Sarah Palin Criticized Over Gabrielle Giffords Presence on 'Target

List,'" Brian Montopoli and Robert Hendin, *CBS News*, January 9, 2011. http://www.cbsnews.com/news/sarah-palin-criticized-over-gabrielle-giffords-presence-on-target-list/

33 Ibid.

34 "Climate of Hate," Paul Krugman, *The New York Times*, January 10, 2011. http://www.nytimes.com/2011/01/10/opinion/10krugman.html

35 "Who is Jared Loughner? Friends Reveal Alienation," *CBS News*, January 10, 2011. http://www.cbsnews.com/news/who-is-jared-loughner-friends-reveal-alienation/

36 Ibid.

37 "Aurora Shooting: ABC's Brian Ross Incorrectly Suggests Tea Party Link," Jack Mirkinson, *The Huffington Post*, July 20, 2012. http://www.huffingtonpost.com/2012/07/20/brian-ross-tea-party-colorado-shooting_n_1689471.html

38 "Batman Colorado shooting: James Holmes fixated by altered states of mind," Nick Allen, *The Telegraph*, July 23, 2012. http://www.telegraph.co.uk/news/worldnews/northamerica/usa/9419299/Batman-Colorado-shooting-James-Holmes-fixated-by-altered-states-of-mind.html

39 "Tamerlan Tsarnaev and Dzhokhar Tsarnaev were refugees from brutal Chechen conflict ," Peter Finn, Carol D. Leonnig, and Will Englund, *Washington Post*, April 19, 2013. http://www.washingtonpost.com/politics/details-emerge-on-suspected-boston-bombers/2013/04/19/ef2c2566-a8e4-11e2-a8e2-5b98cb59187f_story.html

40 "Phone Calls Discussing Jihad Prompted Russian Warning on Tsarnaev," Scott Shane, *The New York Times*, April 27, 2013. http://www.nytimes.com/2013/04/28/us/jihad-discussions-led-to-warning-on-tamerlan-tsarnaev.html

41 Transcribed from video at: http://www.politico.com/multimedia/video/2013/04/wolf-blitzer-talks-about-boston-marathon-patriots-day.html

42 Luke Russert, Twitter post, April 15, 2013, 4:10pm, https://twitter.com/LukeRussert/status/323890994305191936

43 "Matthews Speculates About 'Far Right,' Anti-Tax, Anti-Kennedy Terrorism Behind Boston Marathon Attacks," Andrew Kirell, Mediaite, April 16, 2013. http://www.mediaite.com/tv/matthews-speculates-about-far-right-anti-tax-anti-kennedy-terrorism-behind-boston-marathon-attacks/

44 Ibid.

45 "Remarks by President George W. Bush on U.S. Humanitarian Aid to Afghanistan," October 11, 2002. http://georgewbush-whitehouse.archives.gov/infocus/ramadan/islam.html

46 "Protecting the Force: Lessons from Fort Hood," http://www.defense.

gov/pubs/pdfs/DOD-ProtectingTheForce-Web_Security_HR_13Jan10.
pdf

47   Ibid.

48   "Army Rules That Fort Hood Shooting Victims Will Receive the Purple
Heart," Luis Martinez, *ABCNews.com*, February 6, 2015. http://abcnews.
go.com/Politics/army-rules-fort-hood-shooting-victims-receive-purple/
story?id=28780956

49   "Flashback: What Susan Rice Said About Benghazi," Washington Wire,
The Wall Street Journal, November 16, 2012. http://blogs.wsj.com/
washwire/2012/11/16/flashback-what-susan-rice-said-about-benghazi/

50   "Sources: 3 Al Qaeda operatives took part in Benghazi attack," Paul
Cruickshank. Tim Lister. Nic Robertson and Fran Townsend, *CNN.com*,
May 4, 2013. http://www.cnn.com/2013/05/02/world/africa/us-libya-
benghazi-suspects

51   "CBS transcript: Obama wouldn't call Benghazi terrorism," *USA
Today*, November 5, 2012. http://www.usatoday.com/story/news/
world/2012/11/05/benghazi-attack/1684503/

52   "CBS Says Network President Didn't Influence Coverage Of Brother's
Benghazi Email," Michael Calderone, *The Huffington Post*, May 1, 2014.
http://www.huffingtonpost.com/2014/05/01/david-rhodes-benghazi-
ben-rhodes-white-house_n_5248063.html

53   "Obama: The Vox Conversation," Matthew Yglesias, *Vox.com*, February
9, 2015. http://www.vox.com/a/barack-obama-interview-vox-
conversation/obama-foreign-policy-transcript

54   "Obama's a Fool For Randomness," Jonah Goldberg, "The Corner,"
National Review Online, February 9, 2015. http://www.nationalreview.
com/corner/398258/obamas-fool-randomness-jonah-goldberg

55   "Obama: The Vox Conversation," Matthew Yglesias, *Vox.com*, February
9, 2015. http://www.vox.com/a/barack-obama-interview-vox-
conversation/obama-foreign-policy-transcript

56   "Obama's a Fool For Randomness ," Jonah Goldberg, "The Corner,"
National Review Online, February 9, 2015. http://www.nationalreview.
com/corner/398258/obamas-fool-randomness-jonah-goldberg

57   "Charlie Hebdo editor Stephane Charbonnier crossed off chilling al-
Qaeda hitlist," Lucy Cormack, *The Age*, January 8, 2015. http://www.
theage.com.au/world/charlie-hebdo-editor-stephane-charbonnier-
crossed-off-chilling-alqaeda-hitlist-20150108-12k97z.html

58   "Al-Qaeda Group Claims Responsibility for Paris Terror Attack," Karl
Vick, *TIME*, January 9, 2015. http://time.com/3661650/charlie-hebdo-
paris-terror-attack-al-qaeda/

59   "Democrat congresswoman slams Obama's refusal to say 'Islamic
extremism,'" Cheryl K. Chumley, *Washington Times*, January 28, 2015.

http://www.washingtontimes.com/news/2015/jan/28/tulsi-gabbard-slams-obamas-refusal-to-say-islamic-/#ixzz3QF7bdDf0

[60] "Who's the Enemy in the War on Terror?" Joseph I. Lieberman, *Wall Street Journal*, June 15, 2010. http://www.wsj.com/articles/SB100014240527487035094045753004206688558244

[61] "Remarks at the World Economic Forum," John Kerry, State.gov, January 23, 2015. http://www.state.gov/secretary/remarks/2015/01/236254.htm

[62] "Democrat congresswoman slams Obama's refusal to say 'Islamic extremism,'" Cheryl K. Chumley, *Washington Times*, January 28, 2015. http://www.washingtontimes.com/news/2015/jan/28/tulsi-gabbard-slams-obamas-refusal-to-say-islamic-/#ixzz3QF7bdDf0

[63] Phares, Walid. *Future Jihad: Terrorist Strategies Against America*, Palgrave MacMillan, New York (2005). pp. 142-43.

[64] Ibid. p. 149.

[65] "What ISIS Really Wants," Graeme Wood, *The Atlantic*, March 2015, http://www.theatlantic.com/features/archive/2015/02/what-isis-really-wants/384980/

[66] "State Dept Spokeswoman Marie Harf: We Can't Beat ISIS Just by Killing Them," Andrew Kirell, *Mediaite*, February 17, 2015. http://www.mediaite.com/tv/state-dept-spokeswoman-marie-harf-we-cant-beat-isis-just-by-killing-them/

[67] "What ISIS Really Wants," Graeme Wood, *The Atlantic*, March 2015, http://www.theatlantic.com/features/archive/2015/02/what-isis-really-wants/384980/

[68] Transcription via Daniel Halper, *WeeklyStandard.com*, February 2, 2014. http://www.weeklystandard.com/blogs/obama-999-muslims-reject-radical-islam_836303.html#

[69] "People know the consequences: Opposing view," Anjem Choudary, *USA Today*, January 8, 2015.

[70] "Obama says the Islamic State 'is not Islamic.' Americans disagree." Aaron Blake, *Washington Post*, September 11, 2014. http://www.washingtonpost.com/blogs/the-fix/wp/2014/09/11/obama-says-the-islamic-state-is-not-islamic-americans-are-inclined-to-disagree/

[71] "Islam and the "Killing of Innocents," Dennis MacEoin, *GatestoneInstitute.org*, September 17, 2014. http://www.gatestoneinstitute.org/4702/islam-killing-innocents

[72] Ron George, interviewed by the author at D. James Kennedy Ministries, July 22, 2005

[73] Schmidt, Alvin J., *The Great Divide: The Failure of Islam and the Triumph of the West*, Regina Orthodox Press, Inc., Boston (2004). p. 220.

[74] Robert Spencer, interviewed by Jerry Newcombe at D. James Kennedy

Ministries, August 2005
75 Ibid.
76 Ibid.
77 Phares, Walid. *Future Jihad: Terrorist Strategies Against America*, Palgrave MacMillan, New York (2005). p.18.
78 "The Revolt of Islam," Bernard Lewis, *The New Yorker*, November 19, 2001. http://humanities.psydeshow.org/political/lewis.htm
79 "The World's Muslims: Religion, Politics and Society," Pew Research Center, April 30, 2013 http://www.pewforum.org/2013/04/30/the-worlds-muslims-religion-politics-society-overview/
80 Ibid.
81 Spencer, Robert. *The Politically Incorrect Guide to Islam (and the Crusades)*, Washington D.C.: Regnery. 2005. pp. 114-115. Spencer cites the Haddith book aī al-Bukhārī i, vol. 1, book 2, no. 25 for the Muhammad quotation.
82 Van Til, Henry R., *The Calvinistic Concept of Culture*. Grand Rapids, MI: Baker Book Company. 1959, 1972, reprinted 2001. p. 200.
83 "The World's Muslims: Religion, Politics, and Society," Pew Research, "Chapter 1: Beliefs About Sharia," April 30, 2013. http://www.pewforum.org/2013/04/30/the-worlds-muslims-religion-politics-society-beliefs-about-sharia/#how-should-sharia-be-applied
84 "World Watch List," Open Doors International, https://www.opendoorsusa.org/christian-persecution/world-watch-list/saudi-arabia/
85 "World Watch List," Open Doors International, " https://www.opendoorsusa.org/christian-persecution/world-watch-list/
86 "The World's Muslims: Religion, Politics, and Society," Pew Research, "Chapter 1: Beliefs About Sharia,: April 30, 2013. http://www.pewforum.org/2013/04/30/the-worlds-muslims-religion-politics-society-beliefs-about-sharia/#how-should-sharia-be-applied
87 "Iraqi Christians flee after Isis issue Mosul ultimatum," *BBC News*, July 18, 2014. http://www.bbc.com/news/world-middle-east-28381455
88 "Has Last Christian Left Iraqi City of Mosul After 2,000 Years?," Jonathan Krohn, *NBC News*, July 27, 2014. http://www.nbcnews.com/storyline/iraq-turmoil/has-last-christian-left-iraqi-city-mosul-after-2-000-n164856
89 "The Persecution of Egypt's Coptic Christians," *CBS News*, December 13, 2013. http://www.cbsnews.com/news/persecution-of-egypts-coptic-christians/
90 "Annual Report 2012: Pakistan," Amnesty International. http://www.amnesty.org/en/region/pakistan/report-2012
91 "Pakistan offers little justice for victims of acid attacks," Alex Rodriguez, *Los Angeles Times*, March 20, 2012. http://articles.latimes.com/2012/

may/29/world/la-fg-pakistan-acid-attacks-20120529

92 "Eleven things women in Saudi Arabia can't do," *The Week, U.K,* January 29, 2015. http://www.theweek.co.uk/middle-east/60339/eleven-things-women-in-saudi-arabia-cant-do

93 "Saudi Historian Says U.S. Women Drive Because They Don't Care If They're Raped," Ed Mazza, *Huffington Post,* February 10, 2015. http://www.huffingtonpost.com/2015/02/09/saudi-women-drivers_n_6649896.html

94 "Annual Report 2012: Saudi Arabia," Amnesty International. http://www.amnesty.org/en/region/saudi-arabia/report-2012

95 "Saudi police 'stopped' fire rescue," *BBC News,* March 15, 2002. http://news.bbc.co.uk/2/hi/middle_east/1874471.stm

96 "Crackdown in Iran over dress codes," Frances Harrison, *BBC News,* April 27, 2007. http://news.bbc.co.uk/2/hi/middle_east/6596933.stm

97 "Iran's Headscarf Politics," Fatemeh Aman, Middle East Institute, November 3, 2014. http://www.mei.edu/content/article/irans-headscarf-politics

98 "Boko Haram kidnaps hundreds, tells stories of Chibok girls," Chika Oduah, Associated Press via *Yahoo News,* February 11, 2015. http://news.yahoo.com/boko-haram-kidnaps-hundreds-tells-stories-chibok-girls-111257568.html

99 "The Women of Islam," Lisa Beyer, *TIME Magazine,* November 25, 2001. http://content.time.com/time/world/article/0,8599,185647,00.html

100 "Islamic Extremism: Common Concern for Muslim and Western Publics," Pew Research Center, July 19, 2005. http://www.pewglobal.org/2005/07/14/islamic-extremism-common-concern-for-muslim-and-western-publics/

101 "Rosie O'Donnell, 9/11 Truther and Hater of 'Radical Christianity', Returns to 'The View,'" Scott Whitlock, *NewsBusters.org,* July 9, 2014. (emphasis added.) http://newsbusters.org/blogs/scott-whitlock/2014/07/08/rosie-odonnell-911-truther-and-hater-radical-christianity-returns-vi#sthash.Tb9C0Nus.dpuf

102 "Anti-Choice Violence and Intimidation," NARAL Pro-Choice America Foundation, http://www.prochoiceamerica.org/assets/files/abortion-access-to-abortion-violence.pdf

103 "Abortion clinic gunman dies," *New York Times News Service,* November 30, 1996. http://articles.baltimoresun.com/1996-11-30/news/1996335001_1_john-salvi-ann-nichols-abortion-clinics

104 "Salvi Convicted of Murder in Shootings," Christopher B. Daly, *The Washington Post,* March 19, 1996; Page A01. http://www.washingtonpost.com/wp-srv/local/longterm/aron/salvi021996.htm

[105] "Abortion clinic gunman dies," *New York Times News Service*, November 30, 1996. http://articles.baltimoresun.com/1996-11-30/news/1996335001_1_john-salvi-ann-nichols-abortion-clinics

[106] "Special report: Eric Rudolph writes home," Blake Morrison, *USA Today*, July 5, 2005. http://usatoday30.usatoday.com/news/nation/2005-07-05-rudolph-cover-partone_x.htm

[107] "Appendix A: U.S. Muslims — Views on Religion and Society in a Global Context," Pew Research Center, April 30, 2013. http://www.pewforum.org/2013/04/30/the-worlds-muslims-religion-politics-society-app-a/

[108] "The Future of the Global Muslim Population," Pew Research Center, January 27, 2011 http://www.pewforum.org/2011/01/27/the-future-of-the-global-muslim-population/

[109] "Face the Nation," *CBS News*, November 9, 2009, via "Bob Schieffer on Nadal Malik Hasan: Muslim or "Religious Nut?" on YouTube.com, transcribed by author. https://www.youtube.com/watch?v=LAzw_IJUpEo

[110] "Nidal Hasan convicted of Fort Hood killings," Billy Kenber, *Washington Post*, August 23, 2013. http://www.washingtonpost.com/world/national-security/nidal-hasan-convicted-of-fort-hood-

[111] "FBI official: Hasan should have been asked about e-mails with radical cleric," Carol Cratty, *CNN.com*, August 2, 2012. http://www.cnn.com/2012/08/01/politics/hasan-fbi/

[112] "Senators criticize FBI and Pentagon in Ft. Hood shooting case," Richard A. Serrano, *Los Angeles Times*, February 3, 2011. http://articles.latimes.com/2011/feb/03/nation/la-na-fort-hood-20110204

[113] "Nidal Hasan convicted of Fort Hood killings," Billy Kenber, *Washington Post*, August 23, 2013. http://www.washingtonpost.com/world/national-security/nidal-hasan-convicted-of-fort-hood-killings/2013/08/23/39c468c8-0c03-11e3-9941-6711ed662e71_story.html

[114] Appearance on *Jimmy Kimmel Live*, ABC-TV, January 7, 2015

[115] "Maher vs. Charlie Rose: To Claim Islam Is Like Other Religions Is Naive And Plain Wrong," *Real Clear Politics*, September 10, 2014. http://www.realclearpolitics.com/video/2014/09/10/maher_vs_charlie_rose_to_claim_islam_is_like_other_religions_is_naive_and_plain_wrong.html

[116] https://twitter.com/RichardDawkins/status/552844234689372160

[117] "Remarks by the President at National Prayer Breakfast," The White House, February 5, 2015. http://www.whitehouse.gov/the-press-office/2015/02/05/remarks-president-national-prayer-breakfast

[118] "Inventing the Crusades," Thomas F. Maddon, *First Things*, June 2009.

http://www.firstthings.com/article/2009/06/inventing-the-crusades

[119] "Horse Pucky from Obama," Jonah Goldberg, *National Review Online*, February 6, 2015. http://www.nationalreview.com/article/398030/horse-pucky-obama-jonah-goldberg

[120] Ibid.

[121] Stark, Rodney, *The Victory of Reason: How Christianity Led to Freedom, Capitalism, and Western Success*, New York: Random House (2005). p. 233.

[122] Ibid. p. 9 (emphasis in original)

[123] "Remarks by the President on a New Beginning," WhiteHouse.gov, June 4, 2009, http://www.whitehouse.gov/the-press-office/remarks-president-cairo-university-6-04-09

[124] "Regional Distribution of Christians," from *Global Christianity-A Report on the Size and Distribution of the World's Christian Population*, Pew Research, December 19, 2011. http://www.pewforum.org/2011/12/19/global-christianity-regions/

[125] "Obama on small-town Pa.: Clinging to religion, guns, xenophobia," Ben Smith, *Politico*, April 11, 2008. http://www.politico.com/blogs/bensmith/0408/Obama_on_smalltown_PA_Clinging_religion_guns_xenophobia.html

[126] "Jesus Missing From Obama's Georgetown Speech," Jim Iovine, *4NBC-Washington*, July 13, 2009. http://www.nbcwashington.com/news/local/Jesus-Missing-From-Obamas-Georgetown-Speech.html

[127] "Text-Obama's 2006 Speech on Faith and Politics," *New York Times*, June 28, 2006. http://www.nytimes.com/2006/06/28/us/politics/2006obamaspeech.html?pagewanted=all&_r=1&

[128] "Obama: Sermon on the Mount supports gay civil unions," Michael Foust, *Baptist Press*, March 3, 2008. http://bpnews.net/27532.

[129] "Remarks by the President in Closing of the Summit on Countering Violent Extremism," The White House, February 18, 2015. http://www.whitehouse.gov/the-press-office/2015/02/18/remarks-president-closing-summit-countering-violent-extremism

[130] "Islam In America," *PBS*, http://www.pbs.org/opb/historydetectives/feature/islam-in-america/ via "Obama: Islam 'Woven into the Fabric of Our Country Since Founding,'" Ben Shapiro, *Breitbart.com*, February 20, 2015. http://www.breitbart.com/big-government/2015/02/20/obama-islam-woven-into-the-fabric-of-our-country-since-founding/

[131] "Obama: Islam 'Woven into the Fabric of Our Country Since Founding,'" Ben Shapiro, *Breitbart.com*, February 20, 2015. http://www.breitbart.com/big-government/2015/02/20/obama-islam-woven-into-the-fabric-of-our-country-since-founding/

[132] Kidd, Thomas S. "The Founders and Islam." *Faith and the Founders of*

the American Republic. Ed. Daniel L. Dreisbach and Mark David Hall. New York: Oxford UP, 2014. p. 85.

133 "Egyptian Newspaper's Explosive Allegation," Sharona Schwartz, *The Blaze*, September 3, 2013. http://www.theblaze.com/stories/2013/09/03/egyptian-newspapers-explosive-allegation-president-obama-is-a-secret-muslim-brotherhood-member/

134 Robert Spencer, email communication to author's colleague Jerry Newcombe, February 16, 2015.

135 "Remarks by the President to the UN General Assembly," The White House, September 25, 2012. http://www.whitehouse.gov/the-press-office/2012/09/25/remarks-president-un-general-assembly

136 "Remarks by the President on a New Beginning," *WhiteHouse.gov*, June 4, 2009, http://www.whitehouse.gov/the-press-office/remarks-president-cairo-university-6-04-09

137 "Deciphering Obama in Cairo," Frank Gaffney, Jr., Center for Security Policy, June 5, 2009. http://www.centerforsecuritypolicy.org/2009/06/05/deciphering-obama-in-cairo-2/

138 "Obama: Man of the World," Nicolas Kristoff, *New York Times*, March 6, 2007. http://www.nytimes.com/2007/03/06/opinion/06kristof.html

139 Ibid.

140 "Obama on faith: The exclusive interview," Cathleen Falsani, March 27, 2004. http://www.patheos.com/blogs/thedudeabides/obama-on-faith-the-exclusive-interview/#ixzz3RHVCx0sX

141 Ibid.

142 Ibid.

143 "Remarks by the President at National Prayer Breakfast," The White House, February 5, 2015. http://www.whitehouse.gov/the-press-office/2015/02/05/remarks-president-national-prayer-breakfast

144 "Obama on faith: The exclusive interview," Cathleen Falsani, March 27, 2004. http://www.patheos.com/blogs/thedudeabides/obama-on-faith-the-exclusive-interview/#ixzz3RHVCx0sX

145 "Remarks at the World Economic Forum," John Kerry, *State.gov*, January 23, 2015. http://www.state.gov/secretary/remarks/2015/01/236254.htm

146 Schmidt, Alvin J., *The Great Divide: The Failure of Islam and the Triumph of the West*, Regina Orthodox Press, Boston (2004), p. 17

147 Kennedy, D. James and Newcombe, Jerry, *What If Jesus Had Never Been Born?*, Thomas Nelson Publishers, Nashville, TN (2001), p. 238.

148 Chesterton, G.K., *Orthodoxy*, John Lane, The Bodley Head., London (1909). Long since in the public domain, it has been republished many times and is available online at http://www.gutenberg.org/cache/epub/130/pg130.html

149 "Dem lawmaker blasts 'Professor Obama' as arrogant, alienating," Rep.

Dennis Cardoza, *The Hill*, December 13, 2011. http://thehill.com/blogs/congress-blog/cardozas-corner/198861-the-professorial-president

150 Todd, Chuck, *The Stranger: Barack Obama in the White House*, Little, Brown and Company, New York, NY (2014), p. 489

151 "Subjection to God and Subjection to the State, Part 4," John Piper, *Desiring God Ministries*, July 17, 2005. http://www.desiringgod.org/sermons/subjection-to-god-and-subjection-to-the-state-part-4

152 Reilly, Robert J., *Making Gay Okay: How Rationalizing Homosexual Behavior is Changing Everything*, San Francisco: Ignatius Press (2014). p. 47.

153 Obama, Barack, *The Audacity of Hope: Thoughts on Reclaiming the American Dream*, New York: Random House Large Print (2006). p. 144.

154 Reilly, Robert J., *Making Gay Okay: How Rationalizing Homosexual Behavior is Changing Everything*, San Francisco: Ignatius Press (2014). p. 43.

155 Interview with Jerry Newcombe, D. James Kennedy Ministries, Fort Lauderdale, FL, May 2009.

156 Interview with Jerry Newcombe, D. James Kennedy Ministries, Fort Lauderdale, FL, April 2009.

157 Ibid.

158 D. James Kennedy, "Remembering 9/11," sermon delivered at Coral Ridge Presbyterian Church, Fort Lauderdale, FL, September 11, 2002.

159 "Egypt Conducts Airstrikes on Islamic State Targets in Libya," David D. Kirkpatrick, *New York Times*, February 16, 2015. http://www.nytimes.com/2015/02/17/world/middleeast/isis-egypt-libya-airstrikes.html

160 "Sisi warns of response after Islamic State kills 21 Egyptians in Libya," Ahmed Tolba and Michael Georgy, *Reuters*, February 15, 2015. http://www.reuters.com/article/2015/02/15/us-mideast-crisis-libya-egypt-idUSKBN0LJ10D20150215

161 "Statement by the Press Secretary on the Murder of Egyptian Citizens," The White House, Office of the Press Secretary, February 15, 2015. Emphasis added. http://www.whitehouse.gov/the-press-office/2015/02/15/statement-press-secretary-murder-egyptian-citizens

162 "Obama on Chapel Hill Shootings: Nobody Should Be Targeted Based on Their Faith," Andrew Desiderio, *Mediaite*, February 15, 2013. http://www.mediaite.com/online/obama-issues-statement-on-chapel-hill-shooting-nobody-should-be-targeted-based-on-their-faith/

163 "Brother of two Christian victims of ISIS calls in to SAT-7 live programme 'We Will Sing,'" YouTube, February 18, 2015. https://www.youtube.com/watch?v=-yCmnyzYeW8.

ACKNOWLEDGEMENTS

Though one author's name usually appears on the cover, writing a book is almost always a group project. That is certainly the case with this short book.

First, I am grateful to the Lord for every detail of my life, and for bringing me to D. James Kennedy Ministries in 2001. Working recently under the steady, gracious hand of our president, Jim Carlson, has been a *particular* pleasure.

Thanks to my friend, collaborator, and foil, Dr. Jerry Newcombe, for encouraging me to take this project on. Without his assurances, I likely would not have dared. It was also Jerry who suggested the title.

Though any errors are mine, I am extremely grateful for the supremely professional dedication of Dr. Karen Gushta, whose scrupulous editing made this book much better than it would have otherwise been.

I am thankful for Matt Krepcho, whose boundless encouragement and enthusiasm about this project (which is characteristic of him) pushed me forward. Matt was also kind enough to review the manuscript and offer helpful suggestions.

The tireless and omnicompetent Susan Dzuro read the manuscript and made excellent edits, helping with everything—as always. She also kept things running in our television department while my attention was focused on the book. I literally could not have done this project without her.

Nothing I do would have been possible without my parents, Marlene and Paul Rabe, who have supported and stood behind me since *literally* the very beginning.

Finally—and above all—I am thankful for my wonderful wife Wendy, who has always been my greatest encourager, champion, helper, and love. She and our children, John and Leah, are God's greatest gifts to me, and I shudder to think where I would be without them. Wendy points me to the truth every single day, and everything I have—and everything I do—is better because of her.

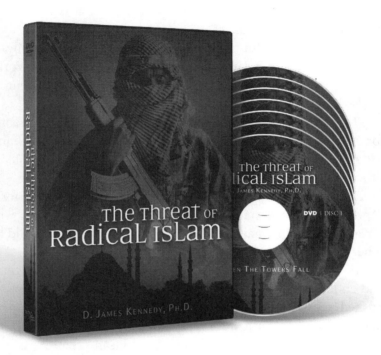

The Threat of Radical Islam

In this set of seven full-length messages, Dr. D. James Kennedy shows the threat everyone—and especially Christians—faces from radical Muslims and explains the danger we are in as a nation if we do not turn to the only One who can be our help and shield.

7 DVD set (720100)
or **7 CD set** (740242)

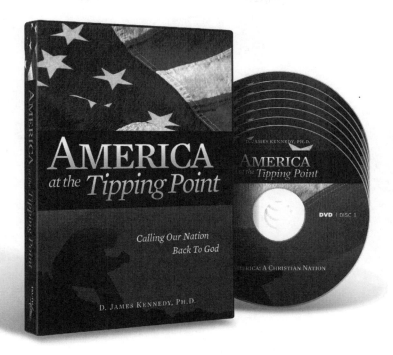

America at the Tipping Point: Calling Our Nation Back to God

These seven full-length messages by Dr. D. James Kennedy lay out America's indisputable Christian heritage and a plan for restoring our religious freedom. Included are: "God and Country," "Spirit of Liberty," "America Adrift," "Returning to Our Roots," and three others.

7 DVD set (720069)
or **7 CD set** (740226)

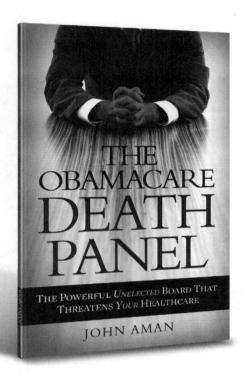

The Obamacare Death Panel: The Powerful *Unelected* Board That Threatens Your Healthcare

Find out what you can do to stop the Government's takeover of your health care decisions by a panel of unelected, unaccountable, non-medical presidential appointees whose decisions have the force of law and cannot be repealed.

Booklet (710019)

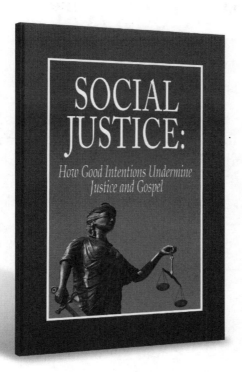

Social Justice: How Good Intentions Undermine Justice and Gospel

One of the foremost evangelical experts on economic and environmental issues today, Dr. E. Calvin Beisner, explains how well-meaning Christians are being duped by those promoting an unbiblical agenda to redistribute wealth under the name of "social justice."

Booklet (115859)

Timely Information and Encouragement!

DON'T MISS OUT...

Sign-up for *IMPACT Magazine and Devotional*, published monthly by D. James Kennedy Ministries.

Enjoy informative articles with biblical perspective on timely topics, find out about new resources the ministry is offering, and follow along daily during each month with devotional material to deepen your understanding of scripture and refresh your soul! All in a beautiful 8½″ x 5½″ digest format.

Visit **www.DJamesKennedy.org** to sign up for the new *IMPACT Magazine and Devotional* today!